From Africa to America

An Immigrant's Story

Eucabeth A Kilonzo

ISBN: 1-4382-4176-3
ISBN-13: 9781438241760

dedication: This book
is dedicated to my parents,
Benjamin and Rebecca Aseno,
who sacrificed everything for my
twelve siblings and me.

Contents

prologue: As a young girl growing up in Kenya, I saw magazines of Andrews University, located in Berrien Springs, Michigan. There was green grass and blossoming flowers in the background, and I would picture myself standing somewhere at the front of the beautiful foliage. I was dreaming that I would someday come to America, further my studies, and make my life worth living.

Earning a good income, supporting my family, and making my parents proud was constantly in my mind. That dream planted in my heart and head has been watered, pruned, and now cultivated. I came to the United States of America from Kenya as a spouse accompanying my husband for further studies, with the hope that I too would pursue my studies. My daily struggles, persistence, dedication, determination, and hard work were my goals, so that I, like many other immigrants who knew that coming to America could be a blessing or a curse, would no longer just dream but see the harvest, a realization in progress a dream with a purpose, a fulfillment.

While in Kenya, I had obtained a Bachelor of Science in Home Economics, with a specialization in Foods and Nutrition. That degree was not an easy achievement; I came from a family of thirteen children, all adults now with Daddy paying all the tuition.

He wanted the best for his children, and that, combined with his insurmountable faith, inspired and reminded me to go above and beyond mediocrity, at home and at school. He retired in my freshman year of college; I was attending an expensive private university and so I struggled, barely holding on to complete my studies. With a passion for learning and a trust in God, I embarked on a Bachelor of Science degree in nursing three years after coming to America, which I completed successfully. Thereafter, I completed a Master of Science degree in Nursing. One dream led to another, and pursuing doctoral studies has been at the top of my to-do list.

Health care is my passion, and so I worked hard to become a nurse. I wanted to serve with a scholarly voice as a health care professional. I knew I could be part of the team that effects changes in these times when we desperately need change, particularly in health care.

I know that I have made the most of opportunities that are not available in developing countries, some of which are stricken by poverty, disease, and civil wars. I must give back now, and I hope my experiences will help someone else pick up the pieces and view with optimism the brighter side of life.

I have had flashbacks of experiences since leaving Kenya, whether in the airplane, in college, or on the streets of Harlem, all part of a dream, *From Africa to America*. The seasonal and climatic differences, and encounters with lifestyle changes, as well as some difficult adjustments to unfamiliar environments, cannot be ignored. Culture shock is a detailed encounter, with comparisons of the lifestyles in the developing countries, to those that are developed. My biggest dream, the nursing experience, is as inspirational as it is motivational to those who aspire to serve in this noble profession. Finally, this is a wholesome account of what the opportunities in America have meant for me and some other immigrants.

The life-changing principles, as outlined here, do not require you to join a weight loss program or visit a psychic. Trying to live by these principles has made my experiences in America worthwhile, and made my dreams the reality that I wanted them to become. With God at my side, without whom I can do nothing, I know facing a *giant* can still be a worthwhile experience. Here is how I have confronted some of the *giants* in the way of my dreams:

1. Sitting around and doing nothing, has never solved anything, even with prayers.
2. This life is about the resolutions you make daily, not annually.
3. Walking costs nothing; sitting can cost you everything.
4. A good attitude makes you do what you imagine impossible.
5. We become what we think most often.
6. Dream positively and make a positive realization out of it. No one can ever dream for you.
7. The sky is not the limit; think beyond the sky.

Journeying to America
"Good-bye"

That Sunday morning anxiety filled the house. The clock was ticking, and time seemed to pass by so fast. The idea of leaving home became a bitter-sweet reality. Bitter because my family was as close as the tongue to the teeth, and separation was but a grim idea. Yet it was, sweet and thrilling because my destination was America, the land of opportunity, money, and freedom to say the least! Still, it wasn't amusing.

I had never been in an airplane before, and as a youngster, I always wondered what gigantic birds they were, but not this time. I was anxious about getting into one. Whatever it was, a Boeing 747 or Air France, what difference did it make? Well, we decided on Air France. "We" meaning my husband and me. He had traveled several times by airplane and it was no big deal for him. We had been married for only five months at the time we left Kenya.

Laughing or crying was a matter of choice when my family, a congregation of Ma, Pa, eight sisters, and five brothers, opened their hymnals and began singing something to the effect of *"till we meet again." The* situation was kind of sorrowful and even mournful at times. I did not concentrate much, participating passively and thinking about the airplane. Soothing anyone did not make sense, and after all, who was going to soothe whom?

As Daddy began pronouncing the last prayer, I said a loud amen, hoping he had finished, and felt quite foolish amid the occasional sobs of my sisters. I then caught a glimpse of my mother's tears, which startled me after a long stare. I began gnashing my teeth to withhold sobbing. I love crying but if I knew I started, it was going to send many a tear rolling.

My family cherished and valued each other, and the bond that held all of us together was our loving, caring, sharing, and treating one another with dignity and respect. This made my departure a difficult experience and as painful as a sore tooth.

On that side of the globe, we have extended families. My maternal grandma is still alive. There are great-grandmas and pas, nieces and nephews, uncles and aunts who can be traced back as far as the late nineteenth century. Yeah! The chain is endless because almost anyone who knows your dad is a relative. They either went to school together or their cattle shared the grazing field. Someone once told me we were related because my great-grandpa was his grandma's boyfriend. With an extended family such as this, I had so many faces to miss. The idea of separation then was not only in my mind; it hovered over my face like a fruit fly. There was a sense of closeness among family, friends, relatives, and even enemies.

After checking in at the airport, it was time to kiss all those loved ones good-bye. I had to bid farewell to Mother Africa, telling her *kwaheri ya kuonana,* meaning, "Bye. I will see you again," and go on my safari. When most Africans hear you mention America or that you are journeying to America, the perception is that "it is the best place" in the world.

Many have the notion that America is a land flowing with milk, honey, and money; and that the dollar is mighty and plenteous you can almost pick it from the streets. Mine, however, was different. I was dreaming of a developed country where I would find the opportunity to better my life, a dream that only I could make a reality.

In the Air

In the airplane, sitting by the window and close to the exit doors, my thoughts were now divided between life in those United States and my pretty mama's face. I had never been far away from home. Moreover, traveling isn't one of my hobbies, as I used to presume, and I wasn't traveling via an automobile or train as I would have preferred. It was approximately twenty-two hours or more by air.

I couldn't figure out the kilometers but I was made to understand that it was thousands of miles to travel. Then, I saw the air hostesses who were moving about, trying to get us to buckle up, their outfits reminding me of the Salvation Army I left back home. Sitting in the second compartment of the airplane, I tried observing everything in view. I was trying to locate the lavatories, which took me quite a while. I had a feeling of urgency, but I tightened my bowels for fear of getting up, and waited, hoping that I would avoid the inevitable. One hostess pronounced that it was take off time and reminded us to buckle up. My belly rumbled loudly as if to compliment the announcement or protest it.

For the first time ever in twenty-five years of life on planet earth, I buckled myself in a seat. I had never bothered myself with seat belts as it was not a requirement in Kenya at that time. Not even as a child was I strapped in a seat. There were no car seats when I was a child. We just traveled, and life continued. I do not know if it had to do with poverty, ignorance, or a lot of faith. Fortunately, it is now a requirement in my country, and hopefully there are minimal fatalities.

I felt so confined on the airplane in a space so small, with so many strangers in seat belts. It was not unusual to have thirty people in a Nissan van or some kind of automobile called *matatu*, traveling unbuckled in my country, with passengers standing out by the doorsteps, trying to hold on to an overloaded vehicle. There would be mothers carrying babies, and old and young people alike. Some people were clean, and some dirty. You could smell them. Plus, there were herring sacks on the roof of the automobile, smelling all the way to your destination, and you would definitely thank God that there was some fresh air in the world when you got out.

My heart was racing and pounding just as hard as my belly. *What a messed up anatomy!* I thought. My anxiety was overwhelming. Cardiovascular-wise, I thought of a heart attack, not that it was in my family medical history, but it was just one of those stupid thoughts we entertain at times. My adrenalin took charge!

My eyes caught the emergency exit doors and were glued there for some time and then shifted to the window, with nothing in view except darkness. It was a darkness that reminded me of the villages back in Kenya with no electricity, where people used kerosene lamps or lanterns at night and had to blow them out by eight o'clock or earlier, for fear of running out of (paraffin) for the next day. And it had nothing to do with the gas prices; it had a whole lot more to do with poverty in a place where some people were so poor, they would rather use the moonlight at night. I cared less for the screen in front of us; to this day, I do not remember what was on that screen. Food was served, and I cannot recall what I ate, either.

Fearful as I was, I could not go to sleep, and my worries ranged from being suspended in the air, to a plane crash or an emergency landing. Even more personal was the idea of persistent fatigue or the thought of what difference an air bag could make in a life-threatening situation. I felt helpless. I wanted to inquire about parachutes but something within told me that would be silly, if not stupid.

Beside the unfamiliar food were unfamiliar faces at the front, back, and sides of our compartment, with the exception of my husband. These are the times when you look at someone and you really do not know whether to smile, laugh, cry, or grimace because you've never seen them before and do not know if you will see them again. So you just pretend you are minding your own business.

Atop the blue skies and clouds over places unknown, the airplane flew, at times in turbulence. I could hardly believe I was thirty thousand feet in the air, traveling at approximately nine hundred kilometers per hour. To me, this was a personal experience, which required no explanation of physics or chemistry. All I cared much about amidst my worries was that America was alive and the pursuit to reach there was deep in my heart. Oh! Bless me, Lord! This was just my flight, my experience.

From Nairobi, the first stop was in Paris, France, and I felt a bit relieved, hoping America was not far off. But by this time, my ears were hurting so bad, and I was afraid to speak up or even cough, because whenever I opened my mouth, all I could hear were loud echoes. However, I was not eager to see France, and moreover, it was raining and dawn. All I saw of France was the airport and a few strangers. We had been sitting for about four hours, waiting for the next flight. I hadn't decided to watch my weight, but there was no smell of French fries anywhere, and I was starved, chewing gum.

The final landing was in Chicago, and I longed to be there but had mixed feelings of course. I was arriving in America but had great sentimentality for Mother Africa, which was now in the distant past yet a precious memory. I had never been away from my parents or siblings, and the comfort and security that home meant were now miles away.

After traveling so long a distance, I heard a soprano voice saying something about approaching O'Hare Airport and mentioning the seat belt again. So tired, worn out, and perplexed, I began looking for the seat belt, forgetting I was still strapped in it, but it was worse. The seat belt and the head phone wires were all tangled up for some reason as I tried unbuckling myself from both. I always thought I was pretty smart but not this time, and one of the unfamiliar faces watched me in disbelief.

Then came the final landing as the gigantic, approximately four-hundred-ton airplane, the one I thought of years earlier as a monstrous bird came down with turbulence and tremors. My heart was racing so fast one could almost see the pumping through my shirt.

The landing was so traumatic, terrible, and devastating or at least I thought so. I was diaphoretic, particularly the palms of my hands, and the rest of my body felt cold, consumed by the tenseness of the moment. When it is your first time in an airplane, you have no comparison to make. I wanted to scream so loud. Then, I had to think about the other passengers who might think I was primitive, not knowing I was flying in the air for the first time from Africa to America.

It seemed the end of my life would be sooner rather than later, and I felt like I was sitting right in a movie theater, watching myself on the big screen in a tragicomedy. My heart was sinking right into my belly, followed by a frightening thud, and I cried inwardly, "*Oh my God! I didn't come this far to be buried!*" At times it is hard to discipline your anatomy, and with all the gastrointestinal problems I had on this airplane, my empty belly screamed one more time in protest!

We finally landed at O'Hare in Chicago. My feet touched the American soil, and I was happy for a moment to be out of that airplane. I was now scared of meeting the man whose story I watched on the news back in Kenya, who had allegedly killed his wife. Just thinking he could still be at O'Hare somewhere hiding was terrifying. Then I learned that there were security cameras everywhere, even on roof-tops, and I was slightly relieved.

As we walked through the aisles to check our luggage, I watched again in disbelief as I saw the biggest dog I had ever seen, with its leash on, and its male counterpart. It went around sniffing the luggage, and I thought. *Wow! There is so much freedom here; even the dogs have some.*

My parents had pets, and from early childhood, I can remember seeing dogs and cats at our house. We were a bunch of animal lovers and took good care of them; Mama baked and broiled chicken for the dogs and cats. The cats drank whole milk while the dogs were neutered. I was little and don't know if dog food existed then.

At my father's home in the village were cows, sheep, chicken, and goats in large numbers. So I pretty much grew up around animals. But this was no petting time. This dog was the last thing on my list of priorities; I was hungry, tired, and felt intimidated. *Why would I carry fish to America?* I thought. *What's the sniffing all about?* I did not smell and had freshened up in France. I felt fresh.

During my childhood, drugs were a mystery. I did not even know anything existed beside aspirin and quinine, which I took when I had malaria in Kenya years back. See, sometimes I take pleasure in being naïve; I had no knowledge of drugs, period, not even at twenty-five years of age. So the dog thing and the sniffing did not make sense to me. There were strangers everywhere too, some smiling, some frowning and a lot more things to see.

We did not stay in Chicago for long, but it was quite a pretty sight, viewing the skyscrapers and having a glimpse of some magnificent buildings. I thought we might have passed by some significant studios. Our final destination was Berrien Springs, Michigan, which would be our home for the next eight years. A friend of ours offered to pick us from O'Hare airport, so we left Chicago forty minutes after landing. A few more skyscrapers reminded me of my beautiful home city of Nairobi, and I just had to sit down and nurse my homesickness.

At three o'clock that afternoon we traveled in a Buick to Berrien Springs, Michigan, where Andrews University is located. The Buick was fancier than our little Honda Civic we had sold in Kenya prior to coming to America. In the back seat of that automobile, I finally went to slumber land. It was time for a long snooze!

Be it as it may, I had been anxious and awake for most of the trip but I couldn't take it anymore. No one resists the beckoning of sleep, even a maniac finds time to snooze, and so I snored all the way to Berrien Springs. Almost two hours of travel were long gone, and my husband woke me up. My eyes opened to lots of stop lights and signs and vehicles. I could barely see any idle bystanders or anyone walking by the roadside like I was accustomed to in Kenya. The roads were tarmac and smooth, unlike the once-familiar little dusty roads. We drove around Andrews University, and it was time to settle to the realities of American life that awaited us, transitioning one day at a time.

The Transition and Encounters

Lifestyle Changes

It was five o'clock in the evening, and to our amazement, the sun was still shining brightly. I wondered why, because back in Kenya, an old mama without a watch could tell the time just by looking at the sun in relation to the shadow. It rose and set at around six every day, and that had been a consistent pattern for as long as I lived in Kenya. We had to adjust our watches immediately since time was no longer the same. Changing the time was perplexing and adjusting the watches disturbing.

Understanding directions was hard enough, but it was a beautiful sight watching the sunset at eight thirty in the evening behind a wooded area off-campus to what I thought was the north but was actually the south. There has never been a sunset at eighty thirty in the evening in Kenya. It would be so dark and most people in the villages without electricity would by sound asleep.

I had learned about the four seasons of North America in high school and was about to experience each season. Mind you, we only have two significant seasons in Kenya, called the wet and the dry seasons. A part of West

Africa has an equatorial climate, and Central Africa has a tropical rain forest. Away from the equator is the savanna, and to the North West there's a Mediterranean climate. We had come to America toward mid-September and it was still quite warm.

Fighting jet lag, we found it strange to be sleeping at eleven o'clock in the United States when previously in Kenya it would be close to dawn, with the sounds of roosters and the hornbill in the villages, and *mataus*, buses, and music in the city. I was in a foreign land where everything seemed so fine yet intriguing for a stranger. We did not know what to expect from the strangers we were yet to meet but at least we saw some smiling faces, which gave us hope for a better tomorrow.

We settled in a one-bedroom apartment on campus that was very costly and that called for *survival for the fittest*. We lived in a large three-bedroom two-bath house in Nairobi after we got married, and as a youngster, I grew up in some big beautiful houses. Back in the village where my dad was raised, there are fading, scant households with grass-thatched mud houses, and of course there are luxurious mansions of pure brick. Believe it or not, not everyone in Africa has "poverty" written on their forehead.

One neighbor could be flushing his toilet while the other goes out to a pit latrine that harbors uncountable flies and lizards, and of course old magazines or toilet paper are choices that have been there. Water also comes in handy and was very inexpensive for my distant Muslim uncle. It is cheaper, of course. He does not have to spend a penny at the giant Naku-Mart in Kisumu for toilet paper.

Then there are a few who prefer to use the bushes; the foliage in the bushes comes in handy as natural wipes. Talk of poverty! The bushes and wooded areas of Africa were at one time considered suitable areas for defecating. Every mile you walked in a wooded area almost guaranteed you would find some human excrement in your path. But that was then, and this is now, and Africa has made so much progress in this area.

If that surprises you, it is called the developing world, where technology or the means to acquire capital is an eternal predicament and has nothing to do with laziness or idleness. It is the truest and purest form of poverty, and most rich people in developed countries can't even imagine it. The bourgeoisies drive the Benz while the common man has cracks on the soles of his feet that a coin can fit in.

In Africa, most politicians are eternally corrupt, thinking of no one but himself, squandering all the aid from foreign countries that can build a nation. The police protection is like betting on your life and it is costly; bribery is all I could think about whenever I saw the police. You can count some children's ribs in some parts of Africa as well as the strands of their hair because of malnutrition, an offspring of poverty. And with such poverty comes the evil combo of disease, civil unrest, and avoidable deaths.

Then there is the other side of the spectrum. The rich who live in mansions and own businesses, private schools, coffee, tea, and pyrethrum plantations; and tons of cows that produce milk of the highest quality. There are people who own homes where each child has his own bedroom, computer, and television. So, on one side of the spectrum is the tycoon, and on the other, the pauper, with little room for anyone called the middle class.

In America, we had to start looking for jobs, not knowing the nature of the jobs that awaited us. We had to work soon enough, whether we liked it or not, to enable us to pay the rent and our personal upkeep, because we came to America independently on no one's terms that meant no stipends or easy scholarships.

Personally, the only job I held in Kenya was at the college cafeteria as a student dietary aide, to assist my retired dad with my pocket money. I was not the only child in college. I would work for an hour or two in the early mornings as I waited for my next class to begin, and that was it. I did not know what working eight or twelve hours straight felt like. Shift work was incomprehensible to me.

I also enjoyed teaching English and history for two months at a local high school while our college went on strike one time, which did not give me enough experience to record it on my resume as an accomplished educator. Other than that, I helped my mom with house chores. Kind, generous Mama did not pay me a penny, and she did not have to. She provided all the necessities: food, clothing, and a roof over my head and they did not ask anything of me.

I was obedient and respectful to my parents, and I respected myself. I was content, and that's all that mattered. I had loving parents, and they were glad to have me. I was in my early twenties, had no driver's license, and was unemployed. Yet some decent clothing and shoes came in handy because over there, your siblings sometimes feel obligated to assist you, and some of mine were well to-do, and so there was minimal peer pressure. I had a lot of beautiful clothes and shoes, and no boyfriends, thank God! It was just a simple fun life for me in my early twenties, with no drugs. I was not glued to the television; it was books that meant everything to me then. Call it the urge to achieve something greater; it was embedded in my soul. Charity had begun at home; where I watched my parents respect and love each other, so there was no need to seek role models anywhere else.

I was raised in a beautiful home, where I could hear my father and mother praying together at six o'clock every morning, sometimes singing, *"Lord, in the morning thou shalt hear my voice ascending high."* It was a team effort, a couple determined to raise their children using biblical standards, teaching us the love of Jesus, which was manifested through their actions of loving God with all their heart and loving their neighbors.

It was therefore easier for us, their children, to follow in their footsteps. They were preaching to us what they practiced, and that is what we all did. By the time I was five years old, we would all be singing on Friday evening to welcome the Sabbath. No work was to be done from sunset on Friday to sunset Saturday. We learned to pray, and even without Mom and Dad at the boarding schools where we studied, we kept on praying. We were not a perfect family, but I cannot lie to you. I love the way I was raised.

I was no perfect woman by any means, either, but my childhood gave me some direction in differentiating between right and wrong which helped me in my teenage and young adult life. I was worse off at ten years old, though.

The problem at that time was snatching a few coins here and there from Mama's business, with my brother, to buy my favorite chewing gum at that time. After taking the coins, we would kneel down and pray not to be caught.

The girls at the boarding school would complain about how terrible their meals were, so one day I devised a plan. I asked my younger sister to carry all of my books in her backpack to give me room to fill my backpack with some home-cooked meals and other food items to take to school and give to my friends. This particular school was closer to home and so we did not board.

The problem was I never asked mama. I was a ten-year-old who was taking coins that did not belong to me. Mama found out what was going on behind her back, any-way; she always seemed to have eyes all over her head. I could never outsmart her. To me, she was a genius who knew me so well and knew everything I did.

Her youngster had become a frequent supplier of groceries to friends at school. She gave me a solid whipping on my behind and reminded me to ask next time. I never repeated the coin-snatching games; I was done! I thought Mama's eyes were similar to a hidden video camera. I was done taking Mama's food to feed the hungry board-ing school girls. To me, this was an act of charity. I had been taught to share and that God wanted us to share with those who did not have. So I did not view my actions as stealing. To me, thieves were big, ugly, and violent men.

I have learnt that my sympathetic attitude is part of who I am, except I do not have to steal anything. I learned of the giving spirit and self-sacrifice early, and even as a child, I thought it my business to take care of people. I always wanted to help someone. I would wake up early to do laundry and other house chores without being asked to do so. Sometimes, it was about volunteering to clean up some old woman's house.

When we were teenagers, Mama warned us about boys. They were off-limits, and so I kind of hated boys instead. They were not to touch me, period. We were supposed to study hard and go to church, and at one point, my sister and I, who were not Catholic contemplated becoming nuns. I believed in abstinence to the point where I thought if my genes were researched for celibacy, the results would skew toward celibate genes. Thankfully, Mama had no need to worry. Sexually transmitted diseases, pregnancy, and acquired immunodeficiency syndrome were realities we only heard of. Thank God for her love and firmness.

The world of today is a very bizarre place. I was sheltered and so I find it hard to comprehend why someone would laugh at a thirty-year old man who is still a virgin. It is like if you have not had sex by the time you are sixteen, then something is wrong with you. And who said everyone should drink wine, smoke, dance, or hang out? There are people who just don't give a damn about some such lifestyles that the majority of children are now craving. Guess who gets the blame? The teachers; why do some parents blame teachers when their children are doing exactly what they see at home?

I was one of the princesses of my father's homestead. We did not go outside to fetch firewood as did other girls. We did not fetch water from a drying river, walk barefooted, or work on my father's huge acres of land during the planting season. Instead, I spent my teenage years indoors, sheltered by a protective, loving, and supportive mother who was raising eight beautiful girls.

We visited the village on several occasions to see Grandma but did not live there; otherwise, we went to boarding schools, and mine was an all girls' boarding school. As for our house, no one bothered my parents with rent or mortgage; they just owned their house on land my father inherited from his father, with no property taxes. I lived there, too. And at least it was big enough to chase my mother's baby girl and even get lost.

Soon I began to notice the vegetation turning red, yellow, and orange. We did not have these seasonal changes in Kenya. A plant was either dried out or green and occasionally had dying or dead leaves. I saw people wearing similar make-up and hairdos in my new environment and I thought, *Wow! How strange! These people have a lot of color going for them.* I was almost twenty six, naïve, and only wore make-up for the first time on my wedding day. Jewelry was not part of my lifestyle, either, no necklaces or bracelets since childhood. We should have saved a lot of money; we did not eat any meat. It was a peculiar lifestyle to many, but we adored it; it was all natural.

Life seemed relaxed and smooth at the beginning of our American adventure. We had paid the first month's rent even though we had no jobs yet. Thank God for a little preparation. We bought a rusted Honda Accord. The good news was it took us places and no one stared at it. I tried hiding while getting into the Honda, feeling a little embarrassed, but most people seemed to mind their own business and that made me feel great.

Groceries were not cheap, and the yellow corn did not taste as good. Indeed, I saw the canned corn in stores in Kenya, but Mama preferred fresh food. She planted corn, kale, tomatoes, cabbage, eggplants, and onions in her big backyard. Truly, it was more of a huge garden, and we picked all these foodstuffs and washed, cooked, and ate them fresh. Fresh food was on our daily menus, not frozen apples.

There were no noticeable sweet bananas in Michigan, and the ones we ate weren't like the tropical ones my mouth knew so well. Sweet bananas are small bananas grown in a place called Kisii in Kenya, and once you eat these, all the other bananas taste stale. We also missed the guavas, and the avocado we bought was tiny and expensive. The avocados grown behind my grandma's house were huge, organic, and delicious!

In my father's house in the village, the barn was right next to the house, and dad employed a herdsman who did all the milking by six every morning and in the evening. For breakfast, we lit the stove, ready to boil the milk fresh from dad's cows, who were accustomed to eating organic grass every day. So I hope you understand when I say that some of the milk we bought from the local stores did not have an authentic taste. I realized I had been drinking organic milk all my life and was accustomed to drinking it without worrying about preservatives or hormones.

I am a vegetarian by choice, or let me say due to my upbringing. Seeing beef that had been frozen for a couple of months or years did not worry me as much as seeing spinach frozen in a box. At eighty-two years of age, my dad visited the hospital for the second time in his life and told us the last time he was hospitalized was in 1946. The man walks every day, and now at eighty-three years old, idleness is not part of him. He walks fast, with no cane or walker, and rides his bike often. His blood pressure is youthful, with no heart murmurs. He loves his Bible, a treasure that probably keeps him going. He is just a courteous, friendly, and loving soul, and so is Mama.

In most villages in Africa, some people still keep chickens in their homestead. When they want to eat chicken, they simply instruct the children to chase the chicken of preference, and within no time, they have the chicken that has been pecking their own corn or worms in their backyard for dinner. These are chickens that have not been subjected to any antibiotics or hormones.

Mama had her own unique ways and schedule of doing things, bless her heart. She is one of the best, most creative cooks, with a variety of delicacies, and I can't even outdo her cooking with my nutrition background. We were a healthy bunch and ate fruits every day. Watermelons and oranges came in handy on Sunday, with bananas on Monday, avocados on Tuesday, papayas on Wednesday, pineapples on Thursday, and a fruit cocktail on Saturday. There was passion fruit and passion fruit juice, black currant and black currant juice, and ribena, which I think still flows in our veins. We lived one of the healthiest lifestyles; I can barely remember any of us getting sick.

Some women teachers at school would ask what we were eating or touch our skin or inquire about the lotion Mama applied on us. Our teeth stayed beautiful, white, and strong from chewing sugarcane, besides using tooth-paste. There were no dental carries and none of my sibling or I had cavities as children. My first visit to the dentist for a dental problem was when I had turned thirty. My teeth were white, except this time I had a cavity that I developed from all the candy from the library vending machine at Andrews University.

Our honeymoon was eventually over, and after a fortnight in America, we got jobs. School began and all of a sudden, almost everything became so involving. My husband was beginning to pursue his studies at the seminary and got a job at the college cafeteria for twenty hours a week, earning four dollars and twenty-five cents per hour. I thought "men die hard" was a statement of significance but not when faced with his occasional groans at night after lifting heavy pots and pans.

His undergraduate course work in Kenya was in theology and had no relationship to the pots and pans he now had to face daily. In fact, he was an associate pastor in one of the biggest churches in Nairobi, but we were here to further our education and better our lives, and washing pots and pans was part of our journey. These are the times the pots and pans become your best friends, because you make a living out of cleaning them.

Real Jobs Don't Come Easy

My job wasn't easy either; my job was beyond my imagination at that time. Unbelievable as it was, what choice did I have? I was not a citizen and probably did not qualify for food stamps, welfare, or any other individual assistance. One thing that I qualified for with certainty was student loans, and I really needed them. With a green card and my enthusiasm for education, this was the best possible dream. I took it seriously not rely on anybody or anything.

I had two hands and feet and no excuse for not working hard. You come to America independently and you have to figure out your sustenance. There is no money in the streets here, only opportunities for the willing mind and soul. I knew God was holding me accountable for the hands and feet He gave me, and I did not want Him to ask me someday what I did with them. There are those who sit and call on His name for rain, but I believe you have to prepare the ground and be ready to plant the seeds first.

I had just completed my course work in Kenya, earning a degree in home economics, but I wasn't going to use it yet. Maybe I needed the pots and pans experience, like my husband, for life's hard lessons, which often shape and refine many lives. I also thought about the graduates in Nigeria who sweep streets to earn a living for lack of jobs. So who was I to idle around or line up for assistance at government buildings with no qualifying factors?

Determined to succeed, I woke up at five every morning and readied for work with a job description that was so difficult to interpret. At first, I babysat fellow students' kids in my own house, and however mediocre the pay seemed, we bought food and underwear.

My first major job was at an adult foster care home where I would assist the elderly with their meals and other activities of daily living, plus some house chores. We did not have such homes in Kenya, and four dollars and eighty-five cents per hour for twelve hours a day, four or five days a week, seemed pretty reasonable fifteen years ago.

I learned from my first day of work that I had not held a real job prior to this one in my short life on earth. At the time I was getting married, my parents were the sole providers of almost everything I owned. I was basically a dependent but going to college at least and not idling in the streets. Daddy had made it crystal clear that education was the key to unlocking life's puzzles and was adamant I had to be in a classroom, learning and fixing my own puzzles, and that idleness did not resonate with him. My tuition was from his wallet and so what alternatives did I have?

In Africa, most eighteen-year-old sons and daughters do not live on their own; it was almost unheard of when I was a teenager. An eighteen-year-old is considered a person who needs direction and guidance, and personally, living with my parents was a joy as there was free food, free clothing, and a free house. I did not have to purchase or pay for anything! I was considered a minor. They were good parents, and I did not see the need to go and live by myself. I would be too scared to try. My mother, being so loving yet protective, could not have fallen asleep at night; even though she knew I was a responsible young woman.

I was so sheltered, and so awful teenage experiences involving drugs and sexually transmitted diseases were not part of my teenage life. I never went to a movie except when I watched Chinua Achebe, the great Nigerian novelist and author, on stage at my high school; neither did I go to any dances. At forty years old, I watched *Fireproof* at the invitation of friends; it was the first movie I ever saw in a theater.

We grew up with firm moral principles, and so a relationship with the opposite sex was out of bounds except for dating and looking forward to getting married. So no intimacy until you say, "I do," was emphasized. Personally, having a boyfriend was not even on the radar in my teenage life, and so when I hear of twelve and thirteen-year-olds having boyfriends and talking about kissing or sex, I get chills.

I was still Mama's big baby girl even in my mid-twenties. I just didn't suck my thumb. Obedience, dignity, and respect for others and me were a must. There were no other options in my household. There are teenagers capable of having self-control, and remember; everyone's life chapter is different. I got to know more about contraceptives ten days before my wedding day when I realized the idea of a baby immediately was not a good one. The nurses at the clinic were laughing and asking me where I had been.

I lived in the innocence or naïveté kingdom. I had a simple, fun life with no TV guiding my morals and teaching me how to be thin and sexy. And if you are not intimate with anyone, why would you be taking contraceptives? Mama was my TV guide, and there was no nonsensical, sexy stuff with her. She was a beautiful woman indeed, who taught me that I was beautiful too and I did not have to try too hard to be sexy to please anyone. She emphasized inner beauty and character, with an emphasis on kindness, gentleness, meekness, faithfulness, love, endurance, and compassion as her guiding principles in training up her children.

She never yelled at us; she was the mama that I had hoped for. So, I felt I owed nobody an explanation for how I looked. It was rather my actions and character and what I did with them that mattered to me, and so I just loved me for who I had always been. I was a pretty woman, but I did not have to wear it on my sleeve. Life was about being more than just another pretty face.

In Michigan, my job title was a *nursing assistant*, and I had never heard of it before. My duties were to bathe eight to ten elderly folk who were wheelchair-bound between six and seven every morning. Readying them for breakfast by 7:00 a.m, was rather challenging and exhausting, and required a lot of lifting. These were activities that were foreign to me. Despite the condition of these dear, elderly people who had aged so gracefully, I took care of them with so much dignity and love. Even the ones who could not speak smiled when they saw me.

Feeding five people all at once, two on aspiration precautions, was long and perplexing, and so was the fixing of nine soaked beds every morning. After this, I washed all the linen, and took the residents back to the bathroom. I took half of them to watch TV and the other half back to their beds for a nap. I mopped the floors and got them all ready for lunch, the wheel-chairs not sparring my legs, sometimes banging me so hard because the job was fast-paced, but I did not complain. I had to work, and it would only take me to kill my dreams. This was not a permanent job. I knew what I wanted for my future, and it was much more.

What was even harder was the fact that I had to see a naked elderly folk. I was not even used to seeing my own husband naked let alone a very old male who, according to my culture was revered and could only be seen naked by his own family. Mind you, I had to bathe and dress these residents and change their diapers, too. Most elderly folk go through the aging process without diapers in Africa. They walk and go to their farms to work. My grandma is ninety-six, Daddy eighty-three, and Mama seventy-six. None of them use a walker or wheel-chair. Grandma has a cane.

See, you might not understand but the elderly in my country are sought for wisdom and are highly respected. They are considered knowledgeable and honored for their contributions in society. There are people who bathe in rivers who do not care about nudity, but we were raised differently. There were showers and bathtubs and no need to use the rivers for my family.

In the evening, sleep was but a dream. I stayed alert most of the night pondering the activities of the day. I had not been exposed to a lot of elderly people who needed so much assistance with almost everything. There were wheelchairs, dentures, diapers, and other prosthesis I had not seen in Kenya.

Most people in Kenya walk, however old, and dentures or any prosthesis are a rarity in Kenya and can be very unaffordable. So brushing and soaking dentures with a tablet was fancily traumatic. We have handicapped people who cannot afford wheel-chairs and some just crawl with their bare hands, feet, or butt on the ground.

In Africa, mainly Kenya, John takes care of his grandpa and Alice her grandma, and so would I. I do not know of any nursing homes in Kenya, and if there are one or two in Nairobi, they are for the rich Asian families who can afford them. As far as I can recall, there were no homes for the elderly in Kenya referred to as nursing homes or adult foster care homes with employees to care of the elderly. If we do have these businesses in Kenya at present, I would like to visit just to compare and have a perspective of the standards of care as a professional registered nurse, since I have said good-bye to my nursing assistant adventure after advancing my education.

In Kenya, each individual family is responsible for their elderly parents or grandparents, to my knowledge. Many people can testify to the fact that they cannot have their parents in a home being taken care of by strangers, and the majority could not afford it, anyway.

I also witnessed abuse in some of the nursing homes as an employee, which was very bothersome. I saw an eighteen-year-old girl mistreating a ninety-year-old man who was unable to button his shirt. Her name was Beanstock, and being raised by a single mom who abused her was no excuse for the cruelty she imposed on this feeble, frail, and harmless old man. This was also the first time I heard of elder and child abuse. I cried inwardly and then out loud to the manager after talking to Beanstock several times to stop. I cannot talk back to my own mom let alone harass my grandma. Discipline was a big deal when I was growing up, and when Mama said something, it was done immediately, with no chance of her ever asking of me to do the same task again.

I knew to clean my room and leave it tidy every morning before going to school, unlike my American-born kids who require a lot of reminding. I live in a culture where I cannot spank my kids, but from my own experience, all the loving spanking my Mama did has made me a responsible human being. It was about being obedient, not stupid. Some scriptures say, "Spare the rod and spoil the child." Others put it this way: *Do not withhold correction from a child, For if you beat him with a rod, he will not die. You shall beat him with a rod, And deliver his soul from hell"* (Proverbs 23:13-14) NKJV.

Mama would use a small stick on the palm of our hands or butt once or twice, and I would never repeat the same mistake again. There were no belts; I did not know that a belt could be used for disciplining a child until a friend mentioned it in North Carolina. No one ever beat me, and why would they? We were well disciplined and cared about our manners. I did not at any time see my parents fight, so I knew not to fight. It was firmness, not laxity, and bringing up permissive children was not on my parents discipline log. Rather, they were guided by the scriptures, and they prayed fervently for each and every one of us, and have not stopped praying for us to this day.

My ninety-six-year-old grandma is still independent and lives in her own house. You would have to literally tie her in ropes to take her to a home full of strangers to live there and be taken care of by other strangers. And if I were to abuse my parent or grandma, no doubt would I live a cursed life for the rest of my days on earth. I learned about this from Exodus 20:12: *"Honor your father and mother, that your days may be long upon the land which the Lord your God is giving you"* NKJV. God commands me to honor them, and I'm sticking with it.

I now know that diapers don't only belong to babies; almost anyone can have a diaper on. Eventually, I quit my job at the nursing home and started seeking employment in a hospital setting as a stepping stone for my future career.

We had encounters with the seasons, as well. The leaves started falling, and they fell day and night. Soon, almost all the trees were naked, and raking leaves became an occupation that many earned dollars from. An African man once came to America in fall. He was shocked to find almost all the trees naked in Michigan, and exclaimed, "Oh! Don't these trees look good for firewood?" Three stones and a fire is a stove for many in Africa, not just a camp fire. Many people in Africa still use wood for cooking and burn wood into charcoal for cooking purposes as well. The warmth diminished, and as the cool air replaced it, the temperatures decreased tremendously and it soon became chilly and cold.

Winter was approaching, and a nice couple directed us to a Seventh Day Adventist community center to get some free warm clothing. These are the times you get those green heavy boots that you dread, but you remain thankful because you cannot afford the black leather ones you would have preferred.

Seasonal Catastrophe

When winter began, I didn't expect the chilling effect. The sun was shining one day, and I couldn't wait to get out of the house to bask. I left on foot for a nearby store, with my free huge green boots, thinking it was warm enough outside, and ended up feeling so foolish. I had to face my ignorance head on and learn from it. I had my coat on but it was literally freezing. With no real winters in Africa, I was not aware of bundling up. I had not learned to pile so many layers of clothing on my body.

My hands began aching, and my ears were hurting. I had not learned that sunshine in winter had nothing to do with warmth. One thing was still missing, though-snow! We only have glaciers on the highest mountain peaks, like Mt. Kenya and Kilimanjaro, so seeing snow fall for the first time was something I anticipated.

We were about to sleep one night when two roaches captured my attention. I did not know I was going to see roaches in America, and here they were not one but two and, boy, weren't they huge! They were chasing each other, having fun, as I waited to smash them. If you do not have the roach spray, you use the shoes sometimes, don't you? The roaches ended up underneath the window sill, and I lost them. As I waited for them to remerge, I saw something white like a pile of clouds by the window. Further down, the ground beneath appeared covered in white. At first, I thought a hail storm was in effect, so I told my husband to accompany me outside.

The chilling effect did not permit us to stay and watch the snow long enough. The snow beamed with vitality, laying on the grass and the pavement, unrelenting. It was a beautiful sight, seeing snow on the ground for the first time. The next day, we had about five inches on the ground and I thought; *it is indeed a blessing that in America even the poorest of the poor can get some warm clothing and boots somehow.* If some snow were to fall in Africa, where unfortunately some people still walk barefoot, people would die like flies.

There were situations, however, that made winter a pain in the rear end. We kept healthy, with no signs of pneumonia or frost bite, but the snow controlled the roads most of the time. There was so much sliding and skidding, one would wonder how many drivers passed the road driving test or got their license from the secretary of state.

There was some frustration behind the wheel, of course. Shame on winter! Frozen bridges, accidents, avalanches and storms! Then there was salt and more salt. The Volkswagen, Cadillac, and a rusted Honda Accord all skidded at the prompting of Mother Nature. I could hardly hear any birds humming outside; someone told me most birds had migrated to Florida.

The squirrels weren't affected; it just seemed like they multiplied and conquered the grass outside instead. It was my first time seeing squirrels. Someone pointing to the squirrels exclaimed, "Oh, aren't they beautiful!" and in a whispered tone, I said to myself, "I haven't decided yet."

Winter wasn't there to stay, and saying good-bye to the salt on the roads and pavement was exciting and relieving. You know, by the end of winter, we had to take the Honda Accord to the junkyard. It was eaten half-way through by salt. The snow and salt does not spare your car unless maybe you drive a Ferrari. I haven't seen a rusted one.

Spring began slowly but carefully, and the temperatures started soaring to the fifty-and sixty-degree mark. The grass regained its color, and flowers blossomed. And one more time, nature's beauty saw a revival. The roads and pavements were free from salt; the coats went back in the closet, and the once naked trees were now adorned with beauty, foliage, and buzzing bees. There was more commotion outdoors, with shouts of joy in the fields, and the playgrounds, which were utilized sparingly in winter, regained full occupancy. Mowing grass rather than raking leaves was the new occupation.

Spring was fine, but no season can ever be perfect; it brought its worries, too. There were some major mosquito bites that one could scratch for days; the good news was that they were not the anopheles malaria-causing mosquitoes. The thunderstorms and flashfloods had a role to play as well, but when I heard of the dreadful scary tornadoes or twisters, there was no tail-wagging for if I were a dog, my tail would be right between my legs. Not that there is no draught in Africa. There are floods that kill people. But I had not witnessed a tornado or hurricane, and watching the impact of Rita on television made my heart pump harder than it did when I was in that airplane.

It was tachycardia, if you know what that means, and it can get worse if uncontrolled.

On CNN, Valerie Voss kept us alive with those "watches." There was flash flood, thunderstorm, and then tornado watches, and all of a sudden, life became so serious for me with minimal smiles and laughter. Shutting all doors and windows and hearing of people running for their lives in the basements or closets made me have nightmares.

I would occasionally dream of a big ball of dark clouds moving over my head in bed, and I would wake up shaking like a leaf with my husband thinking I was having a seizure, which has never been part of my medical history. The thunderstorms clapped harder than any I had ever heard, and the lightning was bright enough to lighten a dark room. I began wondering what my experience was turning into.

I learned about cyclones in geography in sixth and seventh grade but had not experienced a tornado or witnessed any deaths from a tornado in Kenya. The hailstorms in Kenya produced tiny stones almost the size of a peanut and not the giant golf- ball- size hail that fell in Texas, smashing wind shields and causing so much havoc.

The damage from the tiny Kenyan hailstones was only to the crops; no one ever died from them. There are winds that rip off grass thatched roof-tops, and floods that killed people, but no tornadoes in Kenya that I know of that could move houses or cars and twist and smash them in pieces, and kill people.

Summer was jangling! You know, most people assume that Africa's got all the heat. Wrong! I had not been exposed to humidity of such magnitude and intensity as that in Michigan. In fact, I had very limited knowledge of humidity. It was so hot and muggy, I was miserable! Slacks became a rarity, and shorts acquired fame. Some people began walking almost half naked, and it reminded me of someone who had asked if we received our clothes at the airport!

I thought; *you are the one walking naked, not me!* She must have assumed we were had come naked all the way from Africa and received clothes on arrival. Funny, eh! I had not imagined myself sitting on the airplane naked. For most Africans, walking almost naked is not fashionable. It is poverty.

The birth suit is not fashionable to some toddlers who run around in the villages, sometimes sitting on the sand with their bare little butts. This is a catastrophe, and sometimes watching it on the television is only a mere glimpse of a life so real to those who live it daily. The problem is; that's all you see portrayed about Africa on television. No one really cares to show you the beauty that Africa really is. There are some very well dressed people and you can Google Nairobi to see for yourself.

My parents, particularly my dad, worked hard in school and were able to afford clothes, shoes, etcetera, for all of us, so I did not lack anything, and they were kind enough to share their blessings with others. As they taught us, "*He who has a generous eye will be blessed, For he gives of his bread to the poor*" (Proverbs 22:9) NKJV. Furthermore, we did not dwell on material things. Our lives were focused on what was good, what was spiritual. So we felt pity for those struggling daily; it was not a laughing moment for any of us in my family.

In Nairobi, it could get very cold at times, and hot of course, but breezy, with none of the humidity that makes you feel like you're sitting right in between hell and purgatory, if there is such a place. During the months of June and July at the University of Eastern Africa, Baraton, in Kenya, I had to use at least two blankets and a space heater in my dormitory room. It gets that cold in some parts of Kenya, and seven degrees Fahrenheit is not uncommon in Loreto Limuru, a few miles from Nairobi.

My sister studied there and had to carry three blankets to school.

It was miserable indoors and outdoors in Michigan during summer, whereas in Kendu Bay, it would strike eighty-eight degrees outdoors or indoors, yet breezy, and one could sit under a tree and chew some sugar cane, worrying less about a fan or an air-conditioner they could not afford.

Meeting Betty and Amway

At this time, I also met Betty, who made a reference to me being a "little black monkey." It was obvious she despised me, and I thought, *Well, I was not part of the civil rights movement, but someone sure paved the way for me to enjoy some freedom, for which I am thankful, and all I had to do was create peace with my new environment by ignoring her.* If someone were to insist that you are a lion when you know what you are, why argue with them?

I did not come to America by land or sea. I paid for my flight, and the choice of coming to America was my own. I was not going to let Betty be in charge of my life or my dreams. No one ever dreams for me; that was one of my daily resolutions, and it was a resolution for that day. I'm a beautiful black woman, with no monkey business. My family has that soft, silky smooth complexion, and I see it in my American- born kids whom people turn and stare at so often.

What Miss Betty did not know was that my skin bothered her, but I love my skin. It didn't and has never bothered me. It reveals no mosquito bites and doesn't tan at ninety degrees. The doctor might notice the tan; I have not. The difference between me and Betty was that I had more melanin, and if she did not know about melanin, libraries have existed in America for ages. With all the modern technology available, she could have Googled her way to more information.

The animal kingdom has many more differences black, white, red, or brown and they seem to care less. My daddy has cows in all kinds of shades, but they seem contented chewing grass together, never worrying about colors. We appreciate those primary colors in childhood, and if the whole world was all red, I know I would be miserable! I love me black, and I would never wish for any other color on my skin.

I also had an interesting conversation with Delilah. She was wearing some two or three dollar canvas shoes that she had purchased from Family Dollar, and was asking if we have those in Africa. I informed her yes, after which she laughed hysterically and sarcastically, saying she thought most people walked barefooted. How that becomes a laughing matter beats me. She also inquired if I knew Mezz, who lives in Ethiopia, and kept prodding and insisting, "Oh yeah, you must know Mezz." I had never been to Ethiopia, and there could be thousands of people named Mezz around the world. So I just smiled at her and she stopped nagging me.

Ethiopia and Kenya are two different countries, not villages. I also heard someone comment on the continent of Nigeria, and if one can find it on any part of the globe, that person deserves a gold medal. There has never been a continent called Nigeria. All these encounters made me rethink stereotypes. Instead of stereotyping, ask questions, read, or research information. Ignorance in this day and age makes people stereotype, and so exposure can be an excellent learning tool.

A few people were not aware that Africa is the second largest continent on the globe. One person asked me if we lived in trees and did not seem to be referring to a tree house. I told her, "Lady, I come from a family of thirteen children, with Mom and Dad, we are fifteen. How big of a tree do you think would hold us all up there?"

Another encounter was with someone who, intrigued by my accent, asked, "Don't the wild animals create havoc for traffic in the cities?" Well, this gave me an opportunity to explain much of what people do not know about the African continent and the stereotypes. Even as a modern city such as Nairobi, has a backdrop of the beautiful Nairobi National Park, but no lions or giraffes roam the streets. The lions in Africa have never been friendlier. Maybe the mountain lions are a whole lot friendlier, but the African lion rarely leaves any stories to be told in the emergency rooms or trauma centers. When the jungle lions are hungry during drought, everything with blood including the huge elephant becomes dinner.

The media was occasionally frustrating, and I dreaded how Africa was portrayed to the world. It was like there was nothing good over there. Their focus seemed to be on poverty and dirt roads. No one seemed to know the good side of the beautiful continent of Africa. All that was portrayed on the television were riots, killings, and hungry babies, with people making movies and money from some considerably desperate people.

The media misses the mark, there is equilibrium. Besides, there is the Great Rift Valley, the diamonds and gold, organic food, respectful children, professors, engineers and much more. Nothing tastes better than the Kenyan tea which is a major export, and the tourism industry would not flourish if the tourists were just coming to see a bunch of naked people.

I do not know of Africans who have gone to Benton Harbor or Copenhagen and tried to create a movie about anyone or anything. So creating movies with people who did not speak English, people who may never know why their pictures were being taken and may never hear or get to know why the pictures of their naked children were on the screen, possibly without permission, was rather bizarre to me.

I got tired of watching kids with big bellies and flies hovering over and on their noses. This is not a true representation on Africa. Is it not what we do about these pictures that matter? My son, after watching a program of starving children, their ribs countable, told me, "Mama, I cannot go to Africa. I'm afraid I'll die." I had the opportunity to educate him and told him that I lived a good life in Africa and that I was fortunate not to have lived in poverty. Then I used the pictures and the video tapes for visual aids.

I took some pictures of my parent's house and our lovely compound full of flowers and livestock to show him, and his mind has since changed. So far he has made a visit to Kenya, and was in tears at Jomo Kenyatta International Airport on his way back to the United States. He met people who were so kind and loving, and children who did not demand toys. Some could afford to smile in torn pants, contented with the little that was available to them. I know my son's exposure to a different lifestyle will minimize his stereotyping.

There are well-to-do people in Africa and some who do not see flies very often, and even if they do, they mostly live in contentment. *Why can't someone show something good about Africa?* I wondered. Haven't some celebrities built homes in South Africa? Can anything good be said of Africa? Why was there so much concentration on the Rwandan genocide which the international community ignored and most of the world watched in horror doing, nothing?

I got tired of being asked, "Weren't you scared about the civil unrest in Africa?" "Which one?" I asked. I personally did not live to see any, and how many parts of the world can claim true peace? I'm equally afraid of gangs in some neighborhoods and just thankful I live in a relatively peaceful area.

Africa has some booming businesses, with individuals who can afford to educate their children abroad and elsewhere. There are beautiful cities, contrary to most stereotypical ideations of a low lying plain with lots of lions and hyenas. There are huge supermarkets where you can find almost anything. Nairobi, for example is a hub for business and culture, with tourists, suburbs like Runda and Lavington, a sixty-thousand-seat sports stadium, golf courses, clubs, museums, mosques, cathedrals, art galleries, a Hilton hotel, mansions, and slums to name but a few. I come from a large family, and I do not know to this day what it is like to go hungry unless I'm fasting, not starving, and these two are different.

There are some hard-working people in this world who do not just sit and wait for world organizations to hand them yellow corn meal meant for livestock. We do not show the ugly parts of many cities on television to the whole world, yet we are so eager to expose Africa's peril, and sometimes I wonder who is benefiting from that. I would not want my child to be ignorant of the world's geography or economies.

At least we learned about the Great Lakes and the prairies in elementary school, and traveling to parts of Europe, the United States, and Canada besides Africa has made me less ignorant of the world I live in, enabling me to become more appreciative of the cultures represented in this world and therefore stereotyping less. There are some people in North Carolina, and all they know is North Carolina. They have not traveled outside North Carolina and have never been on an airplane before. Since coming to the United States, I have visited at least twenty- five of the fifty states, and I'm gaining knowledge and awareness of my surroundings.

Encountering yard and garage sales was another experience; fifty dollars could buy a whole lot more fifteen years ago. For one dollar, we bought two dishes and another extra two just in case one broke or someone decided to visit. I now missed the dishes we received as wedding gifts; they were countless and you could notice the spirit of giving even from so-called poor people, some of whom had sold their goats or sheep to buy us some dishes.

The yard sales were good in Berrien Springs; I was just disappointed with those who thought they could sell their underwear. Some germs do not die, however hard you try to kill them. Good can also be a relative term when soon we realized that our small apartment had so much junk and we had to dispose of some items from the yard and garage sales.

In the afternoon when I had nothing much to occupy me and I was not working, I would spend time in the mall, admiring what I could not afford and picking only that which mattered. There was an increase in rent for the month ahead and so we got acquainted with credit cards, a bad idea indeed! I had no knowledge of credit cards and interest rates prior to coming to America. I just thought, *Wow! Here is some extra cash I can use to buy a mop and pay back in installments.* I did not know that getting a credit card was like falling into a deep pit with burning coal in it, with a very thin thread to hang onto to get out. The despondency was overwhelming when I learned later about the credit scores, and with a maxed-out credit card and a sixty- day-past-due bill, I had to think quickly.

To make matters worse than they already seemed; we needed a loan to buy another car, which meant borrowing from the bank. I almost felt like there was a huge trap laid before me with huge upper case letters "YOU ARE TRAPPED!" I had promised my daddy and myself that I was going to continue studying to become a successful young woman. I remembered him always telling us that he did not invest in anything other than our education so we could all have a better future. In this nightmare with credit cards and loans, how would that be possible?

In Kenya, we owed no one anything and were debt free, but after settling in Michigan, the mail started coming in with one bill after the other. I had not owned or bal-

anced a checkbook previously so this was tough. I think
after Halloween I got pregnant, so now there was also a
baby on the way. I prayed and hoped that God had spared
us from having twins or I could see myself getting in that
airplane and going back to Africa without accomplishing
my dreams.

My priority of making my life better was not planned
in this order at all: credit cards, loans, and then babies.
But I was determined not to feel helpless or hopeless.
Even though I realized I was in a helpless situation and,
thinking of writing to someone to seek some financial assistance, I decided this was my puzzle to solve and I knew
not to take advantage of anyone.

I chose not to be desperate, and so I worked two jobs
while very pregnant. From an eight-hour job, I would drive
straight through to the next twelve-hour shift. I truly believe that if you have two hands and feet and a determination to live a worthwhile lifestyle, then you will realize
exactly that. We become what we think most often. An
unwilling spirit, laziness, and idleness do not portray lib-
erty to me.

A truly liberated person has to think, regardless of
what part of the planet they come from. We are born with
a mind that should grow and mature daily, and except
for the mentally challenged, we should make appropriate
choices. Sitting around doing nothing has never amount-
ed to anything, even with prayers. I do not for one minute think that God gave us a brain plus those hands and
feet so we should just sit there and do nothing. I had no
room in my mind to entertain excuses! If only.......and if I
was.......No!

Then, we met this couple who introduced us to Amway, a company that was selling household goods. They introduced us to the steps to gaining financial stability and the pyramidal steps to follow to get to the top in that business. This sounded too good to be true, especially when your finances don't seem to add up.

The woman, Mother Theresa, posed like an angel. She said she was going to be our mother. She didn't know that my mama was still much alive and even at close to sixty-four years old at that time was beautiful, graceful, kindhearted, and one of the most compassionate and caring people I knew. Personally, I do not believe in lies, especially from Caucasian Americans; most of the ones I encountered seemed pretty sincere and loving, but we are all human beings and anyone can be a liar. Remember, when politicians lie, it is referred to as misspoken word. How hilarious!

While still battling with "Amway fever," this couple proceeded to sweet-talk us into moving from our apartment, promising that we would move into a nice, clean four-bedroom house with a basement, overlooking a beautiful pond, and would live there free. In return, we would assist by taking care of their elderly parents who owned the house and lived there. Our daughter, Gloria, had just been born two weeks earlier through a C-section. So, this seemed like a brilliant move if we decided to take the offer.

I was on leave, and that meant my husband had to work less besides being a full-time student. Our apartment was too small, and the idea of a big house made us feel lucky, and having no rent very fortunate. And so, my husband and I felt disposed to accept the offer, and together we became a dream team. In the course of the week, we packed our belongings and left for "paradise." One could say we had insurmountable faith, or we were just naïve, or still, stupid. I personally did not see the house before we moved in. So I probably set my own trap.

The house looked ancient yet traditional and beautiful on the outside, and it appeared quite big. The bushes and flowers had grown wild, and the grass was pretty long. Inside the house, I soon became discombobulated. There was a strong smell of kitty feces seeping through the air. Pizza was served but I excused myself. The aroma from the food and the stench from the feces was not a good combination, and I felt nauseated. As a vegetarian, pepperoni was of no use.

I went to change my baby's diaper in one of the rooms and soon started to feel this irresistible itch on my foot. The room had a lit lamp that was dim, and so I went back to the kitchen where there was more light. I saw a flea, then another and another and several more sucking my blood. I was terrified and screamed, "Fleas!" By now I had tears rolling down my cheeks; my life had been that of neatness and now the fleas were sucking away all of my American dreams.

My mother valued cleanliness, and even though she had many children, our house was almost always clean. We washed our bed sheets each week, and every Sunday we aired blankets out in the sun. Hand washing was a must at all times. I remember when we came from school or shook hands with other people; the first thing she said was to go wash our hands.

She feared germs, and even on a clean floor she would tell us to wear shoes or sandals for fear of the germs, but our new found home in "paradise" was so messy, from kitchen to bathroom, and bedroom to basement. I had seen fleas before as a kid, on my uncle's dog. Mama did not allow fleas or lice to come in contact with her children. She tried to protect us from everything: men, mosquitoes, fleas and flies.

We barely fell sick, and if we did, she was there, a nurse herself, taking care of what she could. Our hospital was right in the house, with Band-Aids and all the necessary medical supplies. We only visited the real hospital for major accidents, and fortunately, there were none, and no one in my household suffered from cholera or tuberculosis that required hospitalization. May be there was an appendectomy.

I was not going to close my eyes and fall asleep that night, and the couple knew we were disappointed, but then they left in a hurry for an Amway meeting. We left for the store that night to buy some flea spray to try to kill as many fleas as we could, not that anyone was counting. I felt so trapped. We were up until two in the morning cleaning that house. The following morning, we did more cleaning on the inside and outside, as well as cutting and trimming the bushes.

I was a new mom healing from having had a baby, but what option did I have? Just like Mama, I was not going to let any fleas suck my precious little baby's blood. In college, my room was the neatest. When dignitaries visited the University of Eastern Africa, Baraton, and room fifteen was easy to recognize. Three trophies for cleanliness were part of me. I value tidiness and so I hope you can relate to my torment.

We eventually settled and took good care of the elderly couple, and just as we were trying to move past the flea era, the elderly couple's daughter visited from Georgia. The brother had mentioned that his sister was really mean. She knew how to get in the house because I had the kitchen door open one day as I was cleaning her mom who had gone to the bathroom. I said hello, but she did not respond. She stormed right past me, ignoring me, and with her bare hands, took some wipes, cleaned her mother, and took that pile of feces in the basin; pouring it right into the kitchen sink and through the Sink Erator. I was dumbfounded! We later understood that she was very ill-mannered and did not get along with her brother and sister-in-law who invited us there to take care of their parents. What did that have to do with us?

We did not want to fight with her, it was her parent's house and she was going to do as she pleased, but we were not easily intimidated. Therefore, we made arrangements with campus housing to go back and live on campus. Thereafter, we found acceptance with a loving eighty-eight year-old woman, who was not physically present but conversed with us via phone calls and mail. She became like a grandma to us, calling frequently, and took it upon herself to send us some fifty dollars each month. She passed on, but we will forever be grateful. Our encounters were learning experiences, and we knew we were yet to learn more, including the culture of the environment and the community to which we now belonged.

Culture Shock and Variations

People, Language, Mannerisms

Culture shock: "the confusion experienced when introduced to a culture strikingly different from one's own" (Oxford American Dictionary).

It was time to gain an understanding of a new people, a new environment, and a new culture. I had survived the transition with so much dissatisfaction, and integrating into a foreign culture gave me pangs of fear. Staring at Chicago's splendiferous skyscrapers and driving down LaSalle or Jackson Street was astounding, but this was not my normal environment.

It became difficult trying to distinguish between a city and a town. Seeing signs like Berrien City Limits, I now had to wonder what *city* meant after seeing Chicago and New York. I was so fearful of the bad things America had to offer, yet I knew there were numerous good things-realizing my dreams being one of the good things. I was now part of the land of freedom and great opportunity and prosperity, but I knew it was up to me to choose my destiny.

There were all kinds of people from all walks of life-black, white, and multiracial, as well as Asians and

Latinos-whereas in Africa, it was not a matter of race but tribes. There are approximately fifty to seventy tribes in Kenya alone. The majority of Kenyans are black with varying shades and complexion.

Each tribe has its own unique accent and varied pronunciations. There are a few Caucasians who have made Kenya their permanent home but there are literally no Caucasians or Japanese in the villages as inhabitants. The few you see are diplomats, entrepreneurs, missionaries, or tourists in Nairobi or Mombassa, at the beaches. Some are watching the Serengeti plains and taking pictures of giraffes, or a few are flirting in pubs with beautiful black women. Even more amazing was the fact that I was now considered a minority.

As recorded by Wikipedia, *"By most estimates, Africa contains well over a thousand languages; some have estimated it to have over two thousand languages, most of African rather than European origin. Africa is the most polyglot continent in the world; and it is not rare to find individuals there who fluently speak not only several African languages, but one or two European ones as well."* This is contrary to stereotypical assumptions by most people of a continent so dark with ignorant people, disease, civil unrest, and low intelligent quotients.

It has taken some Rwandese a month or two to learn the English language with fluency. So besides their language, Kinya-rwanda, some Rwandese speaks Kirundi, Kiswahili, and English. It is not bilingualism but multilingualism that is the order of the day in Africa. At age twenty or forty many Africans pick a fourth or may-be fifth language, to include English, contrary to the research that tries to show bilingualism is accomplished with much more ease between ages one and seven.

Thankfully, there was no language barrier for me. I did not have to learn the English language, and even though I had an accent, I spoke the English language fluently. Some people thought I was a fast learner, not knowing I started speaking English as early as preschool in Kenya.

Kenya had been colonized by the British, so, there was no way I could have learned math or chemistry in my mother tongue, which is close to impossible since atoms, and molecules are not found in the Luo dictionary, if one exists. The Luo language is often very easy to learn. Some other African languages are tonal and rather musical, and we thrive on these differences, which we view as social values that make the African continent unique.

Beside English and Swahili, I speak Dholuo as my mother tongue, having been born in Kendu Bay near Lake Victoria, and share a similar ancestry to a famous Luo elder whose son became not a governor but the president of the free world. I'm therefore referred to as *nyar nam*, which means "daughter of the lake," and I'm a Luo, which is my tribe.

Swahili is considered the official language in Kenya. So, it dawned on me that while in America, I was going to be speaking English frequently, but then I thought meditating in Luo would be wonderful since, my husband is from another tribe known as Kamba and we do not speak each other's language. This, however, was not an issue for us.

We were both black and from Africa, and neither Luo nor Kamba was considered a majority. The majority in Kenya is determined by population, not race, because there is only the human race there. The tribe with the highest population according to some recent statistics is the Kikuyu. I also thought that if someone aggravated me, I would respond in Luo or sing out in Swahili. I was stunned and even flustered to hear some English speakers making sentences such as "You was coming to my house."

Socially, *hi* became a familiar word, whereas in Africa, a handshake was the predominant form of greeting and a means of acknowledging someone's presence. Kenyans equally use hugs, but more for close family or friends. You do not hug a king or a queen; you bow your head. As a child, Mom instilled in us some good manners, whether it was in exchanging greetings or in holding conversations, such that profanity, obscenity, and curse words were not part of our daily vocabulary.

There was zero tolerance, so we did not use profanity at home or at school. I therefore felt so lost at the military installation where we were stationed, where profanity came out of some people's mouths with so much ease, including the soldiers that I assumed had all of the discipline one could ever have.

It was sickening hearing the "F" and the "B" word. Shut up! It gave me goose bumps, and the word freaking *sh......*was the major vocabulary at work with professional nurses. My son could not comprehend the ugliness of the word *stupid*, which he heard from another student in his fourth grade classroom.

He was almost in tears as he told me, "Mama, someone at school said the "S" word." He refused to pronounce it, and so I asked him to write the bad word on a piece of paper so I could determine what this bad word was that was tormenting his little mind. Telephone conversations were minimal for me as child, and there were no cell phones then, thank God! It was certainly incomprehensible when my American-born daughter, at ten years of age, asked her father to buy for her a cell phone. *No,* was the quick answer then.

It was interesting getting to know more about a different people, learning about their thought processes, perceptions, opinions, habits, and even body language. I was clueless that individual space ever existed. I was flashing back to my elementary school education, where teachers, parents, and adults were revered, particularly the geriatric population.

I remembered in kindergarten when an adult walked by, we had to stand up, or as soon as the teacher walked into the classroom, we would all be on our feet, chorusing, "Good morning, Mrs. Obudho!" The school uniform was mandatory, and teachers were allowed to discipline kids at school; no one referred to discipline then as abuse.

This modern day thing of kids who are so disrespectful to parents, teachers, and themselves is something I did not see as a youngster, and it is very troubling. We did not call the police when spanked, and spanking in my household meant either your hands or butt was hit once to twice using a relatively thin stick that left no marks or scars. If someone was disciplining me and not abusing me, be it a parent or an administrator, calling 999 in Kenya was unnecessary.

I had no opportunity to watch violence on television and was unaware of child molesters; street gangs, illicit drug use, or drug trafficking. All I knew as a child was that there were thieves who could break into your house and steal your stuff. The police would only be involved with traffic and chasing thieves, and seldom did I hear of a homicide.

Barely anyone owned a gun, and I did not at any time hear of a school shooting. The only shooting I witnessed personally was of a stray dog with rabies at our high school. It was chasing and bit three girls. The dog was resting near my classroom window when the police found and shot it.

In my culture, looking someone right in the eye, especially an adult, was a sign of disrespect or poor manners. I was now in America where I had to look someone in the eye when holding a conversation, otherwise I was considered to be concealing information or being dishonest. This meant undoing my culture to accommodate another. How hard life suddenly became! Some of my Asian friends confirmed that they shared a similar experience. No one was to look at the other right in the eye.

Dress and Obesity

Jeans were on the overwhelming side for me. Not that my brothers did not have a pair or two back in Kenya. But being sort of curvy in my features, I did not wear any jeans and rarely wore pants at all, trying my best not to be the center of unnecessary attention. And as I found out, men here, there, and everywhere are bound to stare at some curves. In America, jeans were the norm. It was more like a uniform that almost every citizen owned, from baby to grandma, and celebrity to pauper in the streets of Harlem, and so I started wearing jeans.

In most villages in Africa, very few girls wear pants, but I've yet to see a grandma in pants. The temperate climate is suited for summer clothes all year long, but the village women do not wear pants, shorts, or miniskirts that expose thighs and bellies. That too is considered disgraceful and degrading; it's a difference in lifestyle. I know of some African women from a particular tribe who would not wear pants, even in the freezing temperatures of Michigan or Minnesota winters.

The elderly village women are very conservative, more or less like the Amish in America. They do not wear tight jeans, mini skirts, or any clothing that exposes body parts. Headscarves, long skirts, and dresses are an asset.

This may sound like a cult to most young people in the developing countries even though it is a cultural difference, and it is very different from a cult or a sect in the African continent. The villagers call it decency. The elderly women are committed to and are concerned with decency, inner beauty, and being appreciated, and would be damned to experiment with superficiality.

Manicures and pedicures aren't a village woman's interest either. Some of them work hard out in the fields and gardens, or they work on pottery, and they barely have money for groceries let alone buying some nails. In Nairobi, however, it is no different than America. It is slowly becoming the little "New York" of Africa. Showing belly buttons and wearing mini skirts and tight jeans are at the peak of fashion now. I could barely wear a sleeveless shirt when I left home. How life can change so quickly.

A striking discovery that caught my attention was obesity, a social problem I was made to understand that made me stop in the hallways, on sidewalks, and in malls-tempted just to stare. Being fat in Kenya is not on the list of social problems or health concerns yet. Of course, we have some overweight people in Kenya, but they are countable.

I truly wanted to be gracious about overweight people since I was raising my own kids who were born in America, and I prayed that they would not gain so much weight that I would stare at them or fail to recognize them from a distance. I would have to allow it to happen by not feeding them right, because the obesity gene does not run in my family or my husband's.

My children eat macaroni and cheese at least six times a year, particularly when I'm so tired from work. I ate spaghetti as a child, but mac and cheese was out of bounds. Red meat takes a long time to digest and so my kids do not eat red meat as long as they are under my roof. For now, it is all about organic and vegetarian foods. Soy milk is as good as they can get, it has never killed anyone. They can decide to enjoy all the meat they want in adulthood, and even then, I'll remind them what their mama taught them in terms of health and nutrition. My chorus is that- this life is all about the daily choices we make.

I watched in distress a day-time show in which a three- or four- year- old weighed one hundred and thirty pounds and I thought of how odd it was that some children in Africa were dying of hunger, yet some children in America were going to die from overeating. How ironic. I saw gymnasiums with so much equipment that I had not seen previously. I just wondered if they were being utilized, because if I were to start a gym business in Kenya, it would definitely be used to keep healthy and very minimally to lose weight. In fact, my gym business might not thrive depending on the location.

Most Africans have such a motile or nomadic lifestyle, and usually the nomads are either pastoralists or peripatetic nomads, and so I found the sedentary lifestyle of most Americans unusual. I would rather watch TV standing and without a bowl of potato chips or popcorn beside me. I was about one hundred and thirty pound, and felt skinny as a woman in America. There were some really big people.

I did not quite understand then how one could get into a car to drive to a store that was four blocks away, paying for gas when walking cost nothing. Of course, we have many genuine idlers in Kenya, but they would have walked for ten miles looking for sugarcane to chew before sitting down by the bus stop to chat, not worrying over a weight loss program or some of the overwhelming diets that don't make sense and which they cannot afford.

That kind of walking, beside poverty and hunger, leaves you no room for growing big or bigger. I had to bathe a woman in a nursing home where I had to lift one fold after another in her belly. I was trying to fit into an environment where everything seemed twice as big: bigger people, bigger cars, and bigger cockroaches.

There are no McDonald's in the villages in Kenya; that business wouldn't thrive. In the Luo communities, people eat fish, collard greens and *ugali* (cornmeal), not sub sandwiches, and with the omega 3's in some fish, some Luo's demonstrate brilliance and excellence in academics, producing the most doctors, engineers, and professors in Kenya. It was something people discussed in schools, and even old grandmas could say, "Fish will sharpen your mind!" It makes you wonder where they did their research.

Many children still walk to school, and previously there were fewer schools, and young children had to walk those eight or ten miles because Daddy had no car to drop them to school in the village and there were no school buses in the villages either. It is different in the cites, however, where there are school buses and regular taxis and rich dad's who can drop their kids to school in a BMW or a Benz. That some children in my new environment would miss school when they were fortunate enough to have the bus stop a few yards from their doorsteps was troubling.

In the forties, my dad was considered lucky because his father was a rich man, and so, he was fortunate to own a bicycle, which he rode for about forty miles to a nice Christian boarding school, where he was taught by missionaries. Most people walked in those days, for ten or more miles, to find a classroom, and sometimes the classroom would be under a tree with a tiny chalkboard, if one existed, and no crayons or textbooks.

Besides, there was rain and the wind or the dust, and crawling insects, all kinds of natural phenomenon to contend with. There are parts of Africa that still experience these conditions. Imagine a classroom with one reading book to share. How about walking to school on an empty stomach or carrying some cold sweet potatoes for lunch and some brown dirty river water as part of this menu for a soft drink? Sometimes we really do not realize or appreciate what we have until we lose it.

Homelessness, Practices, Identification: -No Tattoos, Please!

I was literally in awe when I learned that there were homeless people in parts of Michigan and North Carolina. In Nairobi, the homeless lived on the streets, under the bridges, or in shelters made of plastic bags. And it was not only adults but very young homeless children as well. In the day time, their thin blankets strewn or tacked tightly and packed in dirty plastic bags reminded you that this was another of Africa's perils. At night in the cold or rain, they tried to find comfort and solace under the bridges, some literally savoring the oranges or chicken thighs that lay decomposing in the garbage disposal areas to fill their bellies.

With small empty tin cans, they sat waiting for by-standers to drop a coin or two, or with their hands, half eaten by leprosy laid out; they waited for someone to drop a soft drink or some dry bread. To make matters worse, what remained of a hand without fingers or a foot without toes was a constantly reminder of how painful life can be.

What choice does that give you other than thanking God that you at least have two hands, and feet and could work in a developed country with many opportunities?

In America, not only did I see the homeless in the streets of Harlem, there were homeless people in small parts of Fayetteville and elsewhere. Most of the homeless walked and, had two hands and feet, and so at first I thought this was a hoax. I stretched out my hand and gave whatever I had when I learned it was real for some.

Driving to church on Yadkin Road in Fayetteville, I saw homeless people holding placards in their hands, which said: "Help!" or "Homeless." This was frightening; I had not expected to meet a homeless person in a developed country. The ones that troubled me most were those who would walk by stores or follow you to your car to ask for cash, yet they seemed pretty fine.

Africa is a diverse continent with various cultures represented. With approximately fifty to seventy tribes in a country like Kenya, which is almost as big as Texas, lifestyles vary and there is quite a contrast from one tribe to the next. We speak differently and dress differently, and our meals vary, even in the manner of preparation. The Kikuyu, who live in the central part of Kenya, for the most part prefer *gedheri* (a mixture of green peas, potatoes, and corn) whereas the Luo, who live near the lake, prefer fish. One could say-seems more like environmental conditioning.

The Maasai drink blood mainly from the livestock they own in significantly large numbers. They also drink milk and prefer for clothing their traditional blankets or colorful gear, whereas the Luo's dress extravagantly, wearing suits even on a hot day if they can afford it. Some tribes are athletic, with known long-distance runners, like the Kalenjin's, who live in considerably higher altitudes, whereas some thrive on art and architecture. There are tribal dances, songs, and traditions varying from tribe to tribe.

For most communities in Africa, the birth of a newborn is a celebration and the birth of another community member, and perhaps a future leader, particularly a male child among tribes that are predominantly patriarchic. We have tribes that practice circumcision of all male children, and depending on the tribe or the parents, the procedure can be performed in infancy, early childhood, or early teen years, and there are tribes who do not circumcise at all.

Circumcision is considered a ritual, a passage of rite in which a boy, circumcised at fourteen years of age, enters manhood and is expected to become a responsible team member in that particular community. He learns the ways to manhood, such as hunting, fishing, and farming, being strong, and becoming a provider for a household, not jumping on a trampoline or playing endless games on Play station 3.

It is no secret, however, that some tribes also carry out circumcision for girls, which most Western cultures consider body mutilation. In Kenya, the Kisii tribe practice circumcision of girls, and of course it does not mean all the girls from this particular tribe have been circumcised. And one can make a strong case that breast reductions, breast augmentations, and body piercing are bodily mutilations.

For a part of the world in which there are so many languages, our forefathers came up with various ways of identification. For example, it is easy to identify the Maasai tribe with their long curved ears, ornaments around their upper bodies, and colorful clothing or blankets, which are a major tourism attraction. The Luo tribe, in ancient days, made their identification peculiar by extracting the six lower teeth, so when someone smiled or laughed, one could identify their particular tribe. These practices have become impractical among the Luos with time, even though a few of the geriatric population are easily identifiable by their six missing lower teeth.

My dad had his six lower teeth extracted probably in the forties, but when they got married, Mom made sure he got his fixed. I just never saw him soak his partial dentures with a tablet like I saw people do in the assisted living facilities and nursing homes I referred to earlier. Instead, he brushed them after every meal.

Marriage, Polygamy, and Divorce

Many people wonder about weddings, marriages, and divorce in Africa. Weddings can either be traditional and performed within homesteads or modern in churches. Mine is a Christian background and so is my husband's, and ours was a Christian wedding officiated by a church minister. We had just graduated from college at the time of our wedding.

There were thousands of people seated at church and at the reception. Invitations are not honored by some people and some uninvited guests are bound to show up. It is not easy telling them to leave because in their ignorance, they assume they belong to the community and are there to support you. They do not want to be seated at the wedding party's table, they just want to be witnesses, and a bottle of water or a soft drink might be all they care for at times.

In actuality, we invited four hundred guests, but twelve hundred people showed up at our wedding. I did not wear any traditional clothing as most people speculate; my husband bought my dress in Europe, and I'm one of those who are considered brainwashed by some villagers. I wear pants occasionally when I visit the villages, and that kind of gear is considered Western by some.

An enthusiastic group of young and older women gave a rendition of a typical African dance song for a send-off at our wedding; it was very entertaining. Music and dance plays a significant part in many cultural aspects beside entertainment.

Then, there were those who wanted to eat some real food, and again, we usually try to cook to accommodate such uninvited guests at weddings or funerals. Fortunately, our vegetarian meal stood the test of the multitude that made us very nervous during the reception. Our inviting and accommodating spirit, as well as our courtesy, is noticeable when guests visit our homes. Invited or uninvited, you can guarantee that someone will offer a drink, be it water, tea, or porridge. This is a custom that has been passed on throughout generations.

In the ancient days, however, people eloped, and from talking to some of the elders, there were forced marriages as well, where a man would find a woman, and even without getting properly acquainted or dating for a period of time, he would take her to his home and make a wife out of her.

Elopements, I understand, are common in Western cultures as well. Eighteen- year- olds who decide that they are not going to listen to their parents and marry whoever they have chosen without parental blessings have been aired on some television networks. What if they were ill or demon- possessed? In Africa, marriage is viewed as a unifying force among most communities and joins families and extended families together, so it is not just the two individuals but several others forming a bond, a relation, a community.

In some communities, after a couple makes a decision to get married, there are usually several steps they must take before the actual ceremony. The man visits the woman's home to talk to her parents and get an acceptance or a rejection when he asks for the woman's hand in marriage. The woman also visits the man's home, and acceptance or rejection comes with this visit. If both sides agree, the parents meet thereafter and get acquainted with each other.

This is an opportunity to also study the home and learn about the family mannerisms and religion, or see if there are practices that are incompatible with the other side. Then, the dowry process is initiated, in which the man has to decide the dowry, be it cows, other forms of livestock, or money. As I mentioned earlier, my grandpa was rich, so dad's dowry was sixty cows before marrying my beautiful mother.

Polygamy, an ancient practice, is still alive in some African communities. I count it a blessing that my parents were staunch Christians and so I did not have to worry about having thirty siblings or step- mothers. Mama bore thirteen of us, and my parents' loving, monogamous relationship was something I admired. Even after their marriage of fifty- seven years, they still adore and love each other.

I was so surprised and stunned to watch on television a man forcing fourteen- year- old girls into marriage in a developed country. Some children were being forced into marrying their own relatives or coerced into marrying fifty- year- old men. I have always thought that most Westerners considered polygamy a barbaric practice in the

African continent as a third world's way of life. It is more shocking from an African perspective to see a Caucasian involved with more than one wife and lots of children.

In colonial Africa, it was a black man's thing; the white man had a wife, not wives. During colonialism in Kenya, the British man, the so- called *mzungu*, came with a wife, not wives. So King Solomon in the Bible, I presume, must have been a black man or Middle Easterner with hundreds of wives.

The giving of dowry by the man is still a common practice in Africa and has nothing to do with the buying or selling of a human being. In the Luo culture, dowry is considered as a form of appreciation by the man to the parents of the girl being given in marriage. In the late twentieth century, a man could give to the bride's parents up to sixty or more cattle, mainly cows. In this century, however, the dowry could be limited to ten cows or as few as five in addition to some thousands of cash, but it is different for all cultures represented in Africa. There are tribes who give thousands or more, and yet other tribes only give gifts.

Such traditions are quickly fading in the modern world, where the Western world seems to set a stage for the social events that are more appealing to the younger generations, who are buying into the Western way of life.

The elders of the community are usually invited for the dowry- giving ceremony. Always considered wise, they drill the man to find out if he is going to be a good husband in taking care of the bride. They ask questions about his background to ensure the girl is not being given in marriage to a lunatic, or someone who practices witchcraft. Cohabitation is not as common in African communities;

you are either married or not. An unmarried man, called *misumba,* is kind of looked down on as an outcast in a Luo village.

For centuries, divorce was not a welcome aspect of life in Africa and not as rampant as in the Western cultures, where people marry for a couple of months, days, or hours and then are separated or divorced. Even in crumbling relationships, the couple held on for fear of embarrassment in the community as well as for the consideration of the sanctity of marriage.

It was a major fight, quarreling, or beatings that drove the woman back to her parents to stay there for a while before returning to and reuniting with the abusive husband or not returning at all, a conflict resolution or strategy similar to separation in most Western cultures. Otherwise, couples did not divorce over petty issues such as "Well, baby, you've grown so fat!" There was less cheating, because if a man preferred another woman, they simply married, and he now had wives instead of a wife, and polygamy thrived.

My oldest sister, who is now deceased, was a victim of domestic violence. She was a teacher, her husband a high school principal. They seemed to be in love, but there were problems that my parents would only learn of after she had endured the abuse for almost eight years. Not that she was stupid and could not voice her concerns; she was a brilliant woman who thought the marriage would work and gave it chances, just like many other abused women in our world today.

Our family also took great pride in the Aseno name; Dad had a reputable name as a prayer warrior. His gentleness and compassion was and still is admired by so many, and so my sister kept silent in her agony and pain. My brother- in-law was an alcoholic who grew up in a home where alcohol was brewed by his own mother. The last straw that ended in a separation and eventually a divorce was after she had her fifth child and was expecting the sixth.

The problem at that time was that she was giving birth to girls, and from the husband's perspective, having girls one after the other was enough. He was desperate for a male child, one who would inherit his land and possessions and carry on his name, as was the custom.

What made having girls my sister's problem? They had a big fight one day, in which the man hit her on the head with an arm chair. A gaping wound on her head and blood trickling down her beautiful face and chubby cheeks were now the remnants of a relationship gone bitter, and my sister had to break the silence.

It was on a Saturday morning; I was home with Mama. We were readying ourselves for church when we heard a knock at the door. When I opened the door, my distraught sister stood by the door with a napkin to her head and some blood on her shirt. She wore sleepers, which was unusual because she was always well dressed, and when Mama saw her, they hugged each other and were in tears as Mama whispered a prayer.

I was a minor then and did not learn much of what happened thereafter, but Mama took her to the hospital. Remember, there are no ambulances that pick people from their homes and take them to the hospitals in the villages in Kenya. Daddy had retired and settled on his inherited land, which was in the village. She would later on have a sixth child, who was a boy, while she was still separated from the husband, and they divorced months later.

Gender and Intimacy

Transgenderism, if it exists at all in African countries, is a taboo with risks that are not limited to marginalization and stigmatization. For most families, it is an embarrassment. Some religious fundamentalists condone transgenderism, usually with intolerance. It is more like the voice of one crying in the wilderness; you are already condemned!

Many cultures consider transgenderism a taboo. Then there is also the law that protects not some but all citizens, but ironically, the police do more harm with beatings that are unreasonable. Suffice it to say, to some Kenyan policeman, being transgendered is a crime. And that means, they are coming after you, and the consequences can be tragic. It is prominent in the cities; the villages have limited knowledge of women wanting to be men or vice versa.

The gays or lesbians in the villages are unknown; and there is zero tolerance for two women holding hands or two men kissing in public in the villages. It is not even an issue that politicians have to deal with in their campaigns to win an election. Contrarily, in a huge city like Nairobi or Johannesburg, which are like most American cities, where the youth now watch violence on television, anything is possible. Yet, if there are homosexuals in the city, so much secrecy surrounds the relationship for fear of grave consequences. The African continent is gaining ground in this area. Homosexuality is real in Africa, yet minimal.

Laws protecting minorities like these are rare. These are developing countries where people do not enjoy freedoms like in California, where gay couples go further and perform weddings openly. If Mary were to call Josephine, "my beautiful wife" in public in a village in Kenya, it would be viewed as an obscenity that might incite some stone throwers to act. So far, no one, including the media, has reported on a gay wedding in East Africa. They go to wed elsewhere.

Intimacy for most communities in Africa is a private matter, such that even married heterosexual couples do not display their affectionate gestures of holding hands or kissing in public very often. It is not a society where people fondle and can have sex by the bus stop, like Sweden. For the most part, while in college in Kenya, students appreciated the dark, where most of them did a whole lot of stealing kisses, even in an open relationship.

The watchman was on the lookout, though, as this was referred to as inappropriate behavior among unmarried people and sometimes required visiting the dean's office. Not that this college had lots of teenagers, these were mainly grown men and women, some in their thirties and forties. Some were dating, others engaged.

My parents visited the United States a while back, and we took them to Washington DC for a ride to see the beautiful scenery that included the White House, the Washington Monument, Capitol Hill, and all there is to see in Washington DC. A few yards from Capitol Hill there was a gay party in progress.

My parents had never seen two men or women kiss before and were literally stunned. I said to Mama, "I have not seen two cocks together." Seeing human males fondling and kissing was very traumatizing to her. She usually speaks her mind, but it was none of her business in a country where the lifestyle was different from hers.

My oldest daughter was eight years old at that time; my middle son was five and my youngest daughter two. As a mother, I was and still am very concerned about the world my children are growing up in. My mama cried out loudly for me to run with the children or hide them, and I told her "Mama, this is what goes on in most developed countries that have freedom, and my children, having been born in Michigan, are going to see a whole lot more, which I did not witness in my childhood in Africa."

Growing up as a child, Biblical principles formed the framework of the guiding principles in my family, and so I hope you understand my parents' reaction to homosexuality. They were clueless! If my son came to me and told me he believes he was born a girl, I think I would probably have a myocardial infarction. All the ultra sounds, to my knowledge, indicated he was male, and when he was circumcised, he remained a male child to me. Nothing was altered at birth, and I'm sure when he is in the bathroom, he can figure out his anatomy. I would, however, still love him; he would remain my child forever.

Again, that is my perspective as his mother, having been raised with values and principles that may be different from others. The major problem I have with most African countries is the limited time spent in teaching and educating people about social issues such sexuality, and the rampant spread of a transgendered world that may catch up with the innocent who know nothing. I also understand that so many people, including Christians, have resorted to conforming to the current trends in lifestyles, such that the scriptures are overlooked, and when you speak up then you are referred to as being judgmental.

Most people are comfortable calling a spade a big spoon, unfortunately. As sinful human being, who we all are, I still understand that my Creator made Adam and Eve, not Adam and Steve, and placed them in the Garden of Eden, telling them to "be fruitful and multiply." God himself knew so well where he had placed the reproductive organs.

I also learned about adult toys, I had never heard of them before, and how much some people were obsessed with pornography, and I was thankful that there are very few computers in many homes in the developing countries for this one reason.

I monitor my kids when they are on computers. It is my responsibility. No one is scavenging my children unless I'm deceased. They know the rules already. We are responsible for setting the rules within our household; that is not for the police. Simply put, *"Train up a child in the way he should go, And when he is old he will not depart from it"* (Proverbs 22:6) NKJV.

Death and Dying

What about funerals, graves, and graveyards? When death strikes in most African communities, people cry out loud; they do not sob. Death is the only time we all cry: men, women, and children. There is so much wailing and weeping you could hear the screaming five miles away. You do not hold back your tears; you cry! Some people moan for weeks, even months.

Among the Luo communities, drums are used to alert people of the situation. There is a specific beating of the drums when death occurs. Luo communities do not hold any private funerals, and tens of thousands of people come to the funeral. Visitors and guests travel from all corners of the country on the burial day, and thousands of people are expected, just as it is with weddings and other ceremonial activities. A sense of community and support, they call it, and so lots of cattle are slaughtered, and villagers and visitors are fed.

The majority in Africa are still buried within their homesteads. There are no public or private cemeteries within the villages among the Luo's, and there are very few public cemeteries in the cities that I can recall. Some Muslims cremate; otherwise, unless you are completely burnt in a fire, there are no cremations. Putting ashes in a coffin or in the sea is very uncommon.

Among the Luo's, the man of the household was buried right in the front yard, close to the house, and for some it was a few meters away to the right of the main hut. You own your home. The land title deed is in your name, and you inherited the land, so nobody sets any rules for where you are buried but you. Come on, people, there is some freedom here.

My dad's living will is simple, and it is probably verbal and not written. He will distribute his enormous acres of land to his sons, and he wants to be buried in the backyard of his big beautiful home in the village. How simple! He does not have to pay four hundred dollars to an attorney for a living will. No one gets to fight over jewelry. He has a good watch that my brother's won't fight over.

The man has lots of acres of land and livestock, and he knows who gets what. No one has to tell him. My youngest brother gets the house and the land where dad currently lives. Daddy has no necklaces, bracelets, or earrings, and he never drank a bottle of beer or, wine or smoked pipe in his entire life. Honor is what I see in the man, nothing less. He loves Mama, and never had an eye for another woman. These are the kind of people who deserve a gold medal, but I guess, Dad will get his over yonder when the trumpet sounds and the son of God is revealed in His glory.

Mother wore no jewelry, not even a broken earring fell from her ear lobes. What a choice! It added nothing to what you already were, she said. The eight girls she bore wear no jewelry either, and so the women of the household have nothing to fight over. Mama's clothes are large and almost all of her girls are petite or small, so there are no clothes to fight over, and she is the only one who wears

Cinderella shoes. A simple and a humbling life experience, where materialism has no wings to fly or thrive in the soul.

Usually, the graveyards in the villages are small, and stones are engraved with names and birth dates for those who can afford it. So, you can not pass by a village and see a one- or two- mile cemetery with tombstones and flowers. That too can be very expensive! Most of the cemeteries I saw in childhood were for the Catholic nuns. The cost of a funeral depends on the number of visitors fed. The host cannot expect someone to travel one hundred miles, some riding on their bicycles, and then let them go hungry without providing some food or drink. Other costs could be related to purchasing the coffin; water for cooking, seats for guests, generators for lights or lanterns if someone is poor, a loud speaker or a public address system, and a huge open tent for the guests.

The land is usually free since most burials are within the homestead, so no one saves money for a burial plot, unless they have no land. A five thousand dollar burial plot is equivalent to three hundred and fifty thousand Kenya shillings, enough to bury one hundred people. The government has little to nothing to do with burials or funerals, except for issuing of death certificates.

I once attended the funeral of an elderly friend in Michigan. At the funeral, there were roughly twenty to thirty people, mainly family and friends. No one cried out loudly, and there were a few sobs, with Kleenex readily available. I did not see any one cry out loudly, and I thought that was strange. *These people do not cry!* But it was a cultural difference I was made to understand. We went for the burial as well, and I was shocked that we were not able to view the body before it was laid down to rest. We were told the burial was "private." In Kenya, the body of a deceased is viewed by almost everyone, family, friend, and foe.

Moreover, by the grave side, I was shocked to see a maroon carpet covering the walls of the six-foot- deep grave, which left me speechless. In Kenya, a few graves are cemented, otherwise unto dust you return. And with all due respect, who would be thinking of a carpet? In Africa, most people do not even have carpets in their homes in the villages, much less a carpeted grave!

Landownership and Inheritance

Land ownership and inheritance is widely practiced in Africa. Sons inherit land from their fathers, and so on and so forth. Most people have a home or a house. A home is where your father originally was born in the village; where he might choose to live, return to at retirement, or where he will be buried when he dies. It is very unusual to find a man selling his own home of inheritance. A house might be a temporary place of dwelling like the rental one in the city. One might purchase and own it or leave it when relocating for another job.

In the schools where Dad served as an administrator for many years, the houses for administrators, the teachers, and the staff were free-big, beautiful houses with bath tubs, electricity, and electric ranges, warm water, and mirrors on whichever wall one wanted to view themselves. We even had a water bed. I learned how to bake cakes by the time I was ten. He only paid for utilities, such as water, electricity, and a phone, if there was one. There are a few people who relocate, buying land elsewhere to make a home due to drought in their original homes or to seek a better life in a more business- oriented set-up.

In America, you could have been born in Texas but later on decide to move to New Mexico and buy a home there, and it does not have to be your original place of birth, and you may still choose to be buried in South Carolina. My father will designate land and livestock to my brothers as part of their inheritance. It is a given; they do not have to buy it from him. As for the girls or the women of the home, especially in Luo communities, they usually inherit nothing. Of course, if one has a very wealthy background, the girls may inherit something, but it is very unusual.

Beside, land inheritance is wife inheritance, which is a practice that most people among the Luos find ridiculous and one of the reasons I'm thankful I did not marry from my own tribe. Most Luos do not go by these practices, especially the Christian Luos. When a man dies, his widowed wife, particularly a young wife, is acquired by his brother or a close relative. Some have viewed this practice as a cause for the spread of Acquired Immunodeficiency Syndrome (AIDS) among the Luo's.

Surprisingly, wife inheritance and land inheritance were common biblical practices in Israel in ancient times. *"Moreover, Ruth the Moabitess, the widow of Mahlon, I have acquired as my wife, to perpetuate the name of the dead through his inheritance, that the name of the dead may not be cut off from among his brethren and from his position at the gate"* (Ruth 4:10) NKJV.

Individualism or Disconnection

Individualism is predominant in the developed countries and suits the saying "Everyone for himself and God for us all." You either have a friend, a few friends or none. You can live in a neighborhood where you do not see your neighbor for months, and that is okay and acceptable because you have to mind your own business. Strange!

In the villages back in Africa, your neighbor not only knows you and your children by name but also all the other neighbors, their children, and their grand children. Villagers are never too busy for each other. To some extent, your neighbor is very much your business. You say good morning almost each day and ask about their well- being. If they need help, you step up, too; you are in many ways their 999 because the 999 calls in Kenya are made for the offenders only.

When you knock on someone's door in Fayetteville and find them eating dinner, hearing "Welcome" or, "Would you like to join us?" is rare. And you do not just knock on the door. You must make prior arrangements or call. That is very much unlike Kenya, where you may have to surrender your own plate to a visitor who happens to knock on your door when you are at the table. How can you afford to ignore a hungry woman who has walked twenty miles looking for food?

No man is an island does not apply in most Western cultures. I have found myself in the island situation many times for fear of intruding in someone's space. When my husband deployed in 2003, I was all alone except for my children, who were very young, and my three siblings, who live in other states but called all the time. One of the chaplain's wives did call. I did a lot of crying instead. As someone who comes from a close- knit family, I felt so alone.

Your life is pretty much in your own hands. Some people appear to be living on their own little island. I have not seen my neighbor for three months, and I can not make an effort to knock at the door and just say hello for fear of intruding in his space. Space seems to be a big deal here. My dad would definitely be a mismatch for Fayetteville. Being the friendly man I've known him to be, even stopping pedestrians to say hello and asking where they've come from, he would be in a lot of trouble.

He is very much liked and popular, and some of the pedestrians he has stopped in the past to say hello to were sons, daughters, or grandchildren of friends he attended school with in the, forties. He still remembers their full names. My dad is now in his eighties.

In most Kenyan communities, almost everybody and every child belong to the community. A sense of community and togetherness begins in the household and extends to the community. We have a sense of belonging and friendship that has deep roots throughout so many generations. My parents, for instance, have thousands of friends, and hardly a day goes by without a knock on their door. They are never a lonely pair and there are hardly lonely people.

There are community events, such as fund raising for the less fortunate to send their children to school, and people gladly gather to do so as a community. Some African countries learned the principles of social change a long time ago, which has nothing to do with socialism. You can see villagers stepping up for one another, selling their cattle and even chicken and eggs to raise money to send a child to college. When one arrives in the village to pay a visit, whether bourgeoisie or pauper, it is not about their dollars or shillings, suits or Jeeps.

Most people are happy to see the son of so and so, whose bare butt they saw in childhood, visit the village, driving a Mercedes Benz, and ready to step up to help others. One is probably treated with a whole lot more dignity and respect, if one has these qualities already.

Promiscuity as Fact, or Fiction

Many people have inquired if Africans are more promiscuous, resulting in the deadly AIDS virus that is so rampant in Africa. I sincerely do not know, and some research ought to be done to figure out the promiscuity scale among African men and women in comparison to men and women in other parts of the world. What I know is that we have certain practices in Kenya and Africa as a whole that probably contribute to the many deaths from the Human Immunodeficiency Virus (HIV).

Among them is wife inheritance, which is still practiced by many Luo's most of whom have died in significantly higher numbers compared to other tribes. A woman could also marry a widower whose wife died from an unknown cause only to learn when it is too late that the wife had died of AIDS, and the husband is positive for the virus as well. By then, the woman has contracted the virus and is expecting a second child, the first having died at a few months old of AIDS. The Luo's usually do not circumcise, if that explains anything scientific or not.

We are medically unequipped to handle even malaria in some parts of Kenya, even though the government has

recently sought solutions that include issuing free mosquito nets. There is never enough funding for testing or
educating the people.

From a nursing perspective, we still have public
hospitals that are very inefficient. Patients share beds at
times, and all I could think of was cross- contamination
and transmission of infectious diseases. Most nurses purchase their own gloves, and some small clinics have no
better means of sterilizing equipment than boiling them.
This is the twenty-first century people! In Africa, some
old syringes have been boiled multiple times.

Indeed we have poor people who can not afford
health care and some of the free samples or trial medications cannot reach every sick AIDS patient due to the
poor infrastructure; some roads are impassable. If someone cannot afford medical insurance, antibiotics, other
forms of medications, or good nutrition, the only other
option they have left is death.

With a compromised body and sometimes no good
nutrition, these people die fast. If these people had some
money or medical equipment, could they have lived longer
like their American or European counterparts with the
same disease?

Some of my cousins died in young adulthood, and of
course some of them lying on their death beds waiting to
take that last breath. They would admit that they were not
promiscuous and irresponsible. For some it took that one
time being unfaithful in a marriage or having irresponsible sex to send them to their graves. Thank God for my
firm mother who made it so clear that there was not going
to be any kind of involvement with the opposite sex before

marriage, and that it mattered to my parents what kind of a person their son or daughter was dating. A thorough background check accompanied the dating process.

I passed through the teenage years, and early adulthood like a dream, knowing very little of what teenagers in this day and age know, and I did not miss out on anything! Even better, I slept soundly at night in my own bed till I got married, without worrying about sexually transmitted diseases or AIDS acquired from being irresponsible. For teenagers, I would say wait! What's the hurry? Where did holy matrimony go? I made sure mine was holy, and you can do the same.

When you are brought up with firm guiding principles and counseling, you should count it a blessing. Besides the youngsters we have lost to AIDS, there have been prominent professors, from universities, teachers, businessmen, and women in the statistics of Africa's horror of overwhelming deaths from the deadly virus. So the stagnating economies of African countries are just that, stagnating, because some of the most productive people in these communities are six feet under. Not all of the governments in Africa are irresponsible.

Orphanages that were once utilized sparingly in Africa are growing rapidly and innocent children are left to care for each other the best way they know how, mainly because some daddies could not keep their pants zipped and some mommies lived in the bars, seeking pleasure that never lasted.

No education about HIV/AIDS was offered, and there were no monies to equip the hospitals. Peter could not afford a condom, and John figured out he was dying and still did not care for the Mary's out there, and the cycle of death continues. It is sad indeed that for most of Africa, if it is not poverty, it is disease, and we often battle the two with few or no solutions.

Religion and Voodoos

Africa has religious groups of people who do not believe in the power of contemporary medicine, and people who would not visit the hospital or take medication because of traditional religions, or because they cannot afford it.

One of my great aunts over eighty years of age was bitten by a snake. Whether it was poisonous or not, no one seemed to know, but she applied her own spit to the snake bite and refused any medication or hospitalization. She lived six years after the incident. One could speculate that may be she was smart enough to know that the alkaline content of the saliva could have some neutralizing effect on the acidic venom, or she could have just been ignorant and was spared.

Just like any other part of the world, we have Christians, Muslims, and atheists. There are various religious groups in Africa: Catholics, Pentecostals, Methodists, Baptists, and Seventh-Day Adventists, to mention but a few. There are some traditional religions, too.

Religious freedom is available to most people in the African continent. Children pray at school and say grace for meals in some boarding schools. No Christian school has denied anyone their right to say prayers or call on Jesus' name at school or in government buildings. No one has been quick to rip the Ten Commandments out of any office buildings.

There are Catholic schools, where children go for Mass the first thing in the morning before going to class. There are also Seventh—Day Adventist schools, colleges, and hospitals where prayer is the key to everything. High school kids go out for outreach, preaching in the neighborhoods for those who care to listen, and usually they are in the thousands. Theological seminary students conduct evangelistic meetings often for those who are willing to listen and baptisms are usually in the thousands.

No one is coerced to pray or not to pray, and there are usually thousands of people who show up at such evangelistic meetings. In the hospitals, you will hear some music, and on Saturday afternoon, the youth, church choir, and the pastor may pay a visit at the bedside to sing and pray for the sick. Jesus' ministry in full swing, He never asked permission to heal and pray in the name of His Father.

Oral literature is a significant part of the African culture, and stories and tales were passed on to the next generation by word of mouth. And as such, folk lore, folk tales, and folk music have always been part of the curriculum in the school systems in Kenya. The elderly prefer to tell stories by word of mouth, just as they were passed on from one generation to the next, reminding me of a high school literature trip to a village in Kenya several years ago. It was part of our oral literature class and a worthwhile experience, as well.

It was a team of elderly folk and about twenty students sitting under a tree. They told us stories, one narrative after the other, as they were told in the ancient past, and even more important was the moral behind each story. Story telling has been a way of teaching moral lessons to the young and old alike on the African continent. Proverbs, poems, and alliterations are still widely used.

There are still dozens of witches and magicians, as most people like to refer to them, even though some are psychics, a word less used to refer to the African psychic. There are tribes like the Luo's, that believe in the evil eye theory in which certain people, mainly women, can stare at you for a long time with an evil eye. The evil eyes are believed to penetrate the body and cause side effects, such as a sudden rash of unknown origin, boils, or stomach aches that can eventually result in one's death.

There are Luo's who do not believe in the evil eye theory. The cure is believed to involve approaching the evil- eyed person and asking if she knows of any cures, after which the affected person is considered healed. There are also tribes that believe in evil spirits that can bring bad omen to the community.

One evening after my sister, who was a soloist for the school choir, came home from a choir practice, she told us that they passed by a cemetery for the nuns at a Catholic institution and were warned not to try it ever again at night. Word had spread not to go near the cemetery at night, which was close to the girls' boarding school nearby. My sister was not able to come home one night, so she slept in the dorm. At night, the girls were hearing the same songs they sung that evening being sung by strange voices at a very slow, drowning pace.

Some in the dorms were terrified. There were girls as young as six years old, attending first grade at the boarding school. I went to the same school but did not board. Dad was an administrator in a high school nearby and always picked us up from what was called the evening prep and took us home. When my sister and I went to school one morning, we heard of the girls recounting how one of them had been taken away from her bed by an evil spirit while asleep and ended up in a suitcase storage room that was already locked. One of the girls stated that she felt a hairy something by her bed and was all swollen up when she woke up, screaming.

Then there is a story that was told by my uncle, and may God help him if he lied. It was a story about an evil woman who had died. At night, even before she was buried, people heard strange things, sounds and rattling. He said that when some people went to look at her picture, the pictures instead showed her squinting, mad, and she had overgrown nails. Scary!

There are stories of magicians who could pour water into a basin and call the name of the person they wanted to kill, and the face of that person would appear in the water. After that, the magician would cast a spell, and the victim is believed to have died wherever he was.

And of course, there are night runners. These are people who are believed to run at night, some of them harmless and some harmful. This kind of running is very different from some American who jogs by dusk or dawn, since it consists of intimidation by throwing sand on your roof top or a rotten animal carcass in your yard at night.

What I found peculiar as far as beliefs was a Caucasian nurse telling me at work that if the first thing you meet in the morning is a black cat crossing the road, then you will have a bad day. This is similar to some African cultural beliefs. In the Luo culture, for example, it signifies a bad omen when a black kitty crosses the road right in front of you. I have had so many kitties, black or otherwise, pass in front of me, whether walking or driving, but all I have seen is the Lord's goodness instead. I do not believe in some evil spirit having control of any part of my life.

So I concluded that superstition is multinational and has nothing to do with Africa and voodoism. I have learned that there is not so much of a difference between the witch doctor in Africa and the psychics in developed countries. The psychics may wear different outfits but the practice of calling on the dead grandmas and uncles is the same.

Just be careful next time you look in the eyes of that ninety- year- old African man. Do not stare in his eyes for long, however kind you may be. He will definitely go to his grave with your face in mind for looking him right in the eyes. It spells disrespect to him. Try to cough, hold your breath, or blink if you can afford to. Remember, you can also stare at the flies or the environment.

He was taught and has lived to know oral literature as a way of communication; he associates speech more with the mouth, where the words are coming from, rather than the eyes. And as they say, a blind man cannot look you in the eye, but you can hear him speak. He has nothing to hide.

Economics 101

Wild life, besides agriculture, is one of Africa's economic mainstays. Traveling form Norway or Panama and seeing the wild in their natural habitat can be a great adventure. This is Africa's wild world, the real animal planet, an attraction indeed. We do not often appreciate Africa much until we see a flock of zebras, giraffes, lions, elephants, and tigers, or the ostrich that have lived in the jungle where God meant for them to roam and have a free life. How about the flamingoes of Lake Nakuru?

Africa also has huge game parks and game reserves, where tourists view these animals. There is some beautiful scenery, like the glaciers on Mount Kenya and Mount Kilimanjaro in Tanzania, the Great Rift Valley in Kenya, and of course the magnificent Egyptian pyramids and coastal beaches, to mention but a few.

When it comes to the wild, the Nakuru National Park in Kenya or the Serengeti Plains of Tanzania offers a variety of cheetahs, hippos, lions, and wildebeests. The animal kingdom knows the freedom that mankind longs for. The gorilla is freer in the jungle than John and Jane on planet earth. They do not know the FBI or the secret service. There are no lawyers and no journalists. No living land mammal can claim the giganticness of the African elephant and his freedom of space.

There is a penguin colony in South Africa and a seal colony in Namibia. The nocturnal spotted hyena thrives at Kruger National Park. There are also steenboks and gemsboks.

In Agriculture, the western part of Kenya thrives in growing tea while the north is mainly arid and therefore suited for livestock. But how much can a country rely on rain for its farm produce? When there is drought, it affects both agriculture and livestock. There is also soil erosion and deforestation, and these two affect other economic production, such as forestry and fishing, which in turn breeds unemployment.

The tropical rain forests are found in the high mountains of Cameroon and Angola; the Mediterranean zones are located in North-west Africa. The dry Kalahari and Namib deserts are located to the south west. In manufacturing, crafts are an industry. In mining the Witwatersrand of South Africa is a gold field, while the banks of the Orange River provide diamonds.

Sadly, beside natural phenomenon, corruption and bribery have paved the way to poverty and stagnation in the African economy. Add all this to poverty and disease, and then figure out the instability of the economy in Africa. It has nothing to do with lazy people who do not want to work. There is no welfare program, and most people in Africa walk for miles. A lazy person will not take a ten-mile walk while looking for food.

There are people who have asked me when I'm permanently going back to Kenya despite the fact that I am a United States citizen. I came here in search of a better life, an opportunity to enhance my education. There are so many others who have come for the same reason, even from Ireland and Germany, and I do not know if they have been asked when they are going back. As a nurse in the United States, I have been able to support not only my parents and siblings but others, and despite the weakening dollar and tough economic times, the dollar speaks volumes in developing countries when converted to foreign currencies.

A nurse in Kenya earns approximately two hundred and seventy-five dollars a month, whereas some nurses in the United States earn up to ten thousand dollars a month or more. My children are familiar with the environment where they were born, Michigan. I cannot see my little ones surviving in Kenya for long without a reliable computer and enough books to read. Since I came to America to pursue an education, I would like to share a little of my educational experiences as well.

My Nursing Experience

Oh Hail College!

In the United States, I embarked on my studies, geared toward achieving a Bachelor of Science degree in Nursing. I was moonlighting as a nurse technician, and trying to be a wife, and a mother of to, (an infant and a toddler) as well as a student. I then became pregnant with our third child. It was harder than any path I had previously taken to better my life.

There were those huge medical and surgical text books to study and comprehend, and good or fair teachers in the classroom. There were diapers to change at home, and some very sick patients at work. I also had to keep reminding myself that there was a husband to love and cherish. These are the times when you are close to losing your mind, trying to make ends meet in a foreign country. But then, with determination, hard work, and perseverance, I prayerfully sought strength to keep me going just one day at a time.

Maintaining determination to study and succeed in being all of the above was not easy, either, as stress kicked or just the thought of ensuring that the family was taken care of and still, having a moment to study was difficult. Much of the stress was hidden within my anatomy. As I took that warm shower and got ready to take a nap, the baby would awaken, crying endlessly sometimes. I did not want my husband to know I was struggling to meet all the obligations.

Besides, my friends and some of my classmates considered me a super mom, and I was determined not to let anyone see through my heart and think any less of me. I would take a few minutes to study a few sentences and decide to go to sleep because nothing was sticking in my brain at that time. But as I crawled into bed, there was my husband, wanting to spend the little time I had left with me, and there was an incomplete assignment for the next day to remind me of the tough situation I was really in.

Trying to balance my life around all of my family obligations, chores, and studies was tough. I had to remind myself that there was no longer Dad's wallet to provide for me. Mama and my siblings weren't there to help me this time. This was my cup of tea, and I had to determine how much cream, sugar, or spices I would add to it. Once again, the American dream was far from realistic. I thought of bills, and then phone calls from Kenya, from siblings, cousins, nieces, and nephews who thought I was having a wonderful life in America, and therefore sought some assistance. My nightmare was real, at times obscuring my dreams.

I did not think I was as good of a student as I would have liked to be, and I had a previous love for history that could be traced to third grade, where I listened to fables and folk tales that captured my attention. I remained an excellent history student. My love for nursing was evident however; in the help I tried offering my mom, who was a midwife back in Kenya. She would deliver babies sometimes on our verandah, for teenage girls who could not afford a hospitalization.

Mother assisted freely, never charging anyone for anything. The additional food items and baby clothes offered freely to so many young girls and women from this kind-hearted, caring woman were an inspiration to me at an early age. She was the compassionate nurse I wanted to become, a mentor, and a role model.

When I came to America hoping to further my education, the decision was a hard one but I had to make the choice. With a food and nutrition background, I aspired to become a dietician, yet my caring and compassionate nature led my husband to try to convince me that I could make an excellent nurse. My passion for nursing grew stronger, thinking of my mom, and I knew I would not make many people at a college cafeteria as happy as I would, caring for the sick with compassion. I had two options, though, dietetics or nursing, but one choice to make. I had been in college for four years, and another four was not going to hurt me.

Fortunately, I was able to transfer most of my prerequisites from the University of Eastern Africa, -Baraton, in Kenya, which was affiliated with Andrews University, and so it was going to be less than four years of college, I hoped. I considered a green card a blessing, which paved way to another blessing called student loans.

I would probably still be sitting in a corner somewhere, broken, or flipping hamburgers, and wondering why I came to America. I could have also become an illegal immigrant statistic. But I chose a different path, and believing in God, and being the hard working woman I always thought myself to be, even as a youngster, I thought I would accomplish my goals in America, where opportunity accommodates everyone, regardless of their background or origin.

So when someone talks of race, or says, "I was denied the job because..." I view it simply as an excuse. Of course, racism has not yet been overcome, but I was not paying attention to it because it was a phenomenon that was not really part of my life, having come from a world where there were tribes.

If my current job had a skin color preference to it, I wonder what it would be, but it doesn't. I'm valued for my skills, and the patients are happy to have a skilled nurse at their bedside. They enjoy my accent, and communication has never been a barrier. These patients love the fact that when they ring that call bell, they can count on those who love what they do, like myself, not to waste a minute. Putting a smile on their faces amidst their pain does not cost me a penny.

I love my job, it is fulfilling. I do not see my job as a duty but an opportunity for service. Ensuring that patient safety is my number one priority makes the patient less anxious. The patient can choose not to take Ativan. I do not thrive on mediocrity; I follow rules and prefer paying attention to detail, which in turn gives me the satisfaction to go home after twelve hours of night shift and crawl in my bed knowing I did my very best at work.

I admired and was inspired by the Asians whom I saw in many hospitals serving as doctors. They also operated many businesses, retail and wholesale. I recognized that the majority of the Asians in this country were careful about how wisely they spent their time, and that most of them were intellectually capable and were successful even at school.

It is amazing how, in life, people can take for granted the good that is within their reach. I was not born in America and maybe that gives me the opportunity to open my eyes wider, but no! Who does not know that there is suffering in many parts of the world where children die of starvation? What is so wrong about acquiring some skills to earn a decent lifestyle in a country with overwhelming opportunities?

First, I had to battle chemistry, which I completed successfully. Then, algebra, which I dreaded, except this time, I had to please math, since it was holding the keys to the life I wanted to live, and my dream of becoming a nurse in a country with limitless opportunities.

I lost interest in math in elementary school, because if you did not get it right in class, the teacher would use those firm African bamboo sticks. There was a pile of them in the corner of her office to strike your hands or butt hard. Or she would make you kneel down on the gravel outside of the classroom.

Instead of making me learn, these punishments just did the opposite for me. I did not want anything to do with math, and Daddy, a good mathematician and accountant, sought to help. The improvement was, however, short-lived. In high school, my dislike for math blossomed, and I passed all my subjects, some with distinction, except math.

I had no choice in nursing school and had to learn to love algebra. In fact, it was algebra, which I had failed once in college back in Kenya, that brought me and my husband together. He was just as poor in math, and so the professor came up with this strategy of meeting the three worst students every day at four o'clock for tutoring. One student dropped the class, and there we were, the gentleman that would become my husband and myself, sharing the doomed math class together. Thank God my daughter gets good grades and that we do not have to inherit bad grades.

My final grade was a D or C-, and boy was I glad it was over with till I came to Michigan and had to retake Algebra and make a C or better. I thought. *Well, here comes that demon again!* What did it matter if it was a C+, C, or a C-? It was still a "C." So I used the strategies I applied for the chemistry class. I studied and studied and made the grade, and at least it looked better on my college transcript. I was thrilled, because be it arithmetic or algebra, I had no passion for either.

I excelled in the remaining core courses in the nursing program, some more intense than the others, and held on, because when you have a good dream, you keep dreaming and make the dream come alive for yourself. Just before my graduation, I also tried joining the Army Nurse Corps. I talked to a recruiter and was flown to Detroit, Michigan, for some preliminaries, but I had children and they were my priority.

While a nursing student at Andrews University in Michigan, I had the opportunity of caring for a fifty-one- year- old construction worker who had fallen to the ground while on a roof top and had to have a rotator cuff repair. I had to pre-admit him, go to the operating room, watch the almost four- hour surgery, and help him recover, ensuring that his vital signs were stable. I then cared for him the following day along with the primary nurse. I asked him if he believed in the power of prayer and if it was okay to offer prayers for him. He accepted my request, and so I offered prayers. He smiled, was thankful, and asked if I would be back the following day. It was not just the prayers; he noticed the compassion.

He was readying for discharge one afternoon, and so I helped pack his belongings and educated him on the dos and don'ts for home care. His wife arrived to pick him up as I wheeled him to the car. They both waved and kept saying thank you. I was overjoyed that God had enabled me to take care of a sick person who recognized that I was good at what I was doing, and offered to say thank you. The word *thank you* mean a great deal to me; it was something Mother taught us, and we said it even after eating dinner in Mama's house.

A few days later, during a clinical rotation, the teacher told us over lunch break that she had some good news to share. She said, "*The gentleman Eucabeth took care of wrote to the hospital to thank Eucabeth for the care and compassion she offered while he was hospitalized.*"

I was in awe, and as a student aspiring to excel in my nursing career, this was motivation to last me for the rest of the semester, if not a life time. I have kept that thank you note as a souvenir, and occasionally when I'm having a bad day, I use it as a motivational tool and reinforcement that nursing is about caring and being compassionate in addition to having skills.

The following week did not go as smoothly, even with the new found energy from the thank you note; I ended up feeling so terrible when, on this day, I made my first medication error. Yes, it was not as ugly as a doctor amputating the right leg instead of the left, but when I learned of my mistake, it sent chills down my spine and I began to wonder if I was ever going to be that excellent nurse I dreamt of becoming.

Instead of giving two pills of Cardizem 60mg, I gave one pill of Cardizem 30 mg, which is called an error of omission in nursing lingo. I prefer not to make mistakes, but I learned that perfection is not a guarantee in certain situations. No human being has ever been or will ever be perfect. This day would haunt me for many more days in nursing school and probably thereafter. Other experienced nurses I conversed with tried to offer some encouragement and shared with me some of their worst nightmares as nurses, so there was some reassurance.

There were hills and valleys, good and bad days in my nursing journey. If I told you everything was good and excellent, you would never learn anything as an aspiring student or a new nurse. Occasionally, I do consider myself a new nurse when I have to learn a new concept or reinforce an old one. This had nothing to do with a mistake but just an area of nursing that presents itself quite often.

I had previously seen a couple of dead bodies, but on this particular day, it was my turn to escort a dead body to the morgue. Accompanied by one other student nurse and a security guard, I was terrified of seeing this dead body.

I felt frozen as we wheeled that corpse on the stretcher, thinking, *What if this person is not really dead and starts twitching or talking?* I had seen dead black people, but this was my first time seeing a dead Caucasian. The dead black people, some of whom I knew, had only become darker, even the fairer, more light- skinned had become truly black. The Caucasian, on the other hand, turned very pale, with bluish- purple or blue lips, and I was scared!

Trying to remove a ring from a dead person's finger or brushing their hair made me have palpitations that would have required a heart monitor. I would occasionally shake like a leaf as the security guard opened the cold doors of the morgue, not knowing what to expect.

The morgue itself was freezing, and I couldn't wait to get out and never return, feeling that all my nerves were on edge. If only I could brush my nerves to calm me down! Seeing more corpses' feet was even more daunting, and making me want to scream were those body parts piled in biohazard bags. My eyes caught a glimpse of an amputated leg, and I said to myself, *I have to get out of here!*

I now began to think deeply that nursing was not just about giving medication, or delivering babies. Rather, it was a world of knowledge where you would still remain in touch with reality, and offer compassionate care to the schizophrenic screaming a mouthful of foul language while you had to remain calm. Treating the patient as an individual and with all the dignity affordable was a must.

It was the real world, where you take care of a fellow human being, and often try to remember what it would be like in their shoes. It was also a profession ruled by critical thinking and skills, with no room for poor decision- making or judgment, or the use of mere emotions as part of problem- solving.

I also learned that this was a profession where, if you are caring, and unfortunately not all nurses are caring people, sometimes you find yourself lost in the caring of others and can forget yourself. Taking a break or going to the bathroom becomes a task you do not want to deal with, and no one pays for the consequences but you. One of the consequences for some nurses has been a urinary tract infection. Peeing is a luxury on busy wards with very sick people, and so is taking a break for a sip of water. One can easily become dehydrated.

The Nurse

After graduation, more hurdles remained. I had to prepare to take the National Council Licensure Examination for Registered Nurses (NCLEX-RN), or what is often referred to as the State Boards exam. I did not celebrate much for my graduation because passing this exam is the only thing that truly qualifies you to have a license to practice as a registered nurse. I kept checking the computer for my results, and so when I saw my license number on the computer screen on the third day after taking the exam, I was thrilled.

I knew I was a registered nurse, and my name had an additional title to it. It would read as Eucabeth RN. My dream had matured into reality, and so I kept going back and forth, turning the computer on and off, and just getting excited at the reality of seeing my license number all night long, and not forgetting to thank my creator. I was a nurse; yes, I was a registered nurse! I had just realized one of my dreams, and no one would deny me the excitement.

The six weeks of internship ended rapidly, and boy did I find myself on my own! The complexities of caring for a cancer patient were mind-boggling. It was a retired member of the faculty of Andrews University with lymphoma and other complexities. She had a colostomy bag that I had to completely empty the contents of every now and then, and as I worked on the bag, carefully emptying its contents, her frail body tried to force her eyes open, concentrating on my face and hands.

I can assure you it wasn't the fresh aroma of Chinese fried rice, but I gave her a smile in return amidst the odor that had now filled her room, and was quite significant in the hallway. It is called humility, and it enables you to treat the patient with dignity as well as remain the professional you have been trained to exemplify. We were warned in class never to make faces at vomit, feces, or odorous wounds. How about just being a human being with compassion!

After accomplishing my task, she felt nauseated, asking feebly for an emesis basin. I grabbed two towels, placing them on her torso while I raced for an emesis basin. I gave her another smile when she was done vomiting. She smiled back and said, "Thank you." I said to my self, *if I could handle six to nine patients with similar problems like these each night I came to work, I would truly be the nurse human resources and the patients sought.*

The night, however, was not promising for a new graduate nurse with nine sick oncology patients on neutropenic precautions, and problems ranging from insomnia, pain, shortness of breath, nausea, vomiting, diarrhea, and impending codes. I bothered other nurses, asking questions for all the help I could get, and was glad that I made it through that first night, thank God!

The following day, I admitted a patient who had gone through chemotherapy and was in the final stages of her battle with lung cancer. I had learned that one of the side effects of chemotherapy is alopecia, but for some reason my patient's name was hard to determine as male or female, and her voice sounded hoarse and deep from radiation therapy.

On entering her room, I said, "Good evening, Mr. Concord!" And the next thing I heard was, "Miss, not Mr." I apologized but lived with the embarrassment for so long. And sometimes you think it only gets worse. Suddenly came the dreaded call in the middle of changing that bed pan that one of my patients was short of breath; I prefer the nursing term *dyspnea*. You really have to be swift, sharp, and skilled to handle the fast-paced nursing care units where patients are so sick and can code on you in a matter of seconds.

How was a fresh college graduate to handle that? Of course you panic, but then you also think, *it is my license, and I'm not going to lose what I just finished working so hard for*. I prioritized my care by asking the nursing assistant to complete the bed pan emergency. I asked the unit secretary to call the respiratory therapist as I assessed the patient and called the doc. We managed to stabilize the patient, thank God!

Code Blue and the Elderly

One afternoon after receiving a report from one of the nurses, I went to assess one of the patients who had just been admitted thirty minutes prior to my shift. I reported to work, and the nurse before me had tried to stabilize him. While performing the initial assessment, I noticed bounding pedal pulses, dyspnea, and incoherent speech, and notified the respiratory therapist after noticing on pulse oximetry; an oxygen saturation of 82 percent. He had been placed on two liters of oxygen per nasal cannula, which I increased to four liters, as his breathing was shallow.

While I was at the desk paging Dr. Guptaka, his mother came rushing out of the room and screamed, "He does not look good! "When I rushed back to his room, his pupils were fixed and he was gasping for air, and so I called a code.

I had witnessed a code, but had not participated in one, and I was one frightened nurse. I had never seen a doctor drenched in sweat, trying to save another human's life before. We often do not give some of them the respect they deserve, do we? Some of the malpractice law suits do not add up. I performed CPR for the first time; my heart beating like it was going to stop, even though I seemed to be doing fine. The successful resuscitation was completed, and it was time to rush this patient to the intensive care unit.

Accompanied by the health care team, we were literally running with the stretcher in the hallways when this gentleman attempted to code a second time. As I continued to give him air via an ambu bag-what is referred to as bagging, I felt some wetness on my pants. I had forgotten I was on my menses, and it was now dripping on my sock, but I had to take care of what was most important first: a human life. I would deal with my embarrassing emergency later.

Occasionally, there would be that geriatric patient who just wanted a listening ear and would hold that lengthy conversation with the list of accomplishments, which included World War I, World War II, and Vietnam. Or it would be about how hopeless life has been since he lost his dear wife. Who would not want to listen to someone who has contributed to the freedom we all enjoy, and at least say thank you.

I would then be ten minutes late giving medication to the next patient, and my manager would be contemplating what to do with that tardy. If a patient still has a mouth, let him talk. Illness does not make a person less human and two or ten minutes late, that is not jeopardizing the next patient, but is spent reassuring the other has no negligence attached to it.

How about the ninety-three-year- old Alzheimer's patient who has just figured out he can dig through his feces, smearing it all over his face, hands, and everywhere, including the telephone. We call it "code brown" on my floor. I cannot afford to leave them unattended. Someone has to care for this old lady, and that person is me, so I go in there with all kindness and humility, the smell of feces having been part of my career for fifteen years, and clean them up good.

You talk of nurses being paid well; that's a bad joke. This is a job that requires your whole being: mentally, physically, spiritually, and emotionally. This job can be overwhelming to some, and there are nurses who have walked through those hospital doors never to return.

The Art of Caring

The art of caring for human beings with dignity when their body system is compromised, and they are not their authentic self is an astounding experience that requires a lot of patience and critical thinking skills. I have worked in various specialties and moved to various parts of the United States. Truthfully, the reward of knowing that you served a fellow human being with dignity and respect fills your heart when you go home in peace, knowing you did the best you could to make a difference in someone feeling his worst.

It is good to know that even when the patient is in a contact isolation room, coughing up blood from tuberculosis or having a fever from H1N1, they still got the best care from another compassionate human being. The gentle touch of a caring nurse goes a long way to provide hope, beside a prescribed medication that might only relieve the symptoms.

A few years after my graduation, I decided to take a critical care course. I watched a coronary artery bypass graft (CABG) that lasted approximately five hours, after which I followed the patient to the floor and assisted with the admission and assessment.

This was a cardiothoracic intensive care unit where, as a nurse, you are introduced to more intense skills and you get to see more medical and hemodynamic monitoring equipment. I had previously worked with patients on ventilators, and so the vent was not a big deal. I was trying to familiarize myself with arterial lines and swanz- ganz catheters. Seeing it in class and applying the skills to a patient were two different things. The ICU comes with tons of challenges, including sicker patients, hemodynamic monitoring, sepsis, third-spacing, and drug overdose, to name but a few.

Occasionally, there is that gun shot patient, a burn victim, and a snake bite victim. In nursing practice, I took care of a young teenage girl who had been shot at a shopping mall. I thought the media craving to get her story was a tragedy in itself. All that this youngster required was to breathe and get some quality care. All that mattered was that she survived and needed to heal.

I never knew I would be privileged enough to work for Uncle Sam and take care of soldiers, some with C4 shrapnel wounds on post and others returning from the combat zones in worse conditions, most of them young and suicidal.

I once took care of a suicidal female soldier who had taken multiple medications. She wanted to die. The beautiful twenty- three- year- old, now lying in bed, appeared to be here only in body. Several nurses gathered by her bedside. She was very combative at first, hurling curse words as we transferred her from the ER gurney to her bed. She hit and spat, vomited, and pulled her intravenous lines out. Doctor's orders for a restraint were available, and we had to tie her to her bed for her own safety as well as the staff's safety. She was one strong woman, but it was painful hearing what she had to say.

Several hours after she had calmed down and the restraints were discontinued, she told me, "Yeah, I know you guys are trying to help me, but no one can help me. I was in Iraq and watched one of my friends beheaded. Now if you think I can live with that; then think again. I will eventually kill myself." The nurses on this shift remained calm and provided reassurance. It is a team effort that ensures the safety and quality of care for a patient, regardless of her condition. A unit guard had to stay at her bedside all night and the following day, she was transferred to a psych unit for further evaluation.

If I were starting my career over, I still believe I would choose nursing as a career path. Just being there and talking to someone from your heart, manifested in your actions, letting that person know you care, and that his well-being is important to you is a rewarding experience.

Are you considering nursing as a career path? Know your passion, and then ask yourself if that is the best possible thing you could do. Let caring be at the top of your list, not how much money you will be making. Review your personality in relation to your career before enrolling in school for three years without deciding your career path. There are people who drop out in their third year of college undecided. How beneficial is that? Time wasted can never be regained. Let no one tell you otherwise. We only live one day at a time, and if it was your twenty- first birthday today, tomorrow you will have to add one day to it.

Personally, nothing has been more rewarding than becoming a professional nurse. America provided that opportunity, and I went for it. It is not when opportunity knocks your door; it is when you knock on opportunity's door that you find some meaning in life.

Working hard and harder, I now can sign my name as Eucabeth RN, MSN, and even with all the other academic credentials behind my name; I am still striving for academic and professional excellence, to continue serving fellow human beings. For me nursing equals service. This is a privilege and an honor for me, and when I become Eucabeth RN, PhD I will not cease dreaming. Where God has not limited me, I'm not limiting myself. I have set my goals way higher. Indeed, the sky is the limit for most people, but I try to set my goals way beyond the sky.

Making the Most of Opportunity

Education

Most Africans hunger and thirst for school. They long to be educated, but the majority has not always had the opportunity or the means to get into a classroom and get the education of their dreams. Growing up, Daddy took it upon himself to reinforce in each and every one of his children an appreciation for learning, and getting educated.

One of my mom's cousins was a graduate and a high school teacher, and seeing her pictures in her graduation gown and hood was inspiring and motivating to me as a child. I told my parents that I wanted to study so hard like Aunty Tabitha. Most girls during Aunty Tabitha's days in school were either married or only completed fifth or sixth grade if they tried hard enough.

My major dream for coming to America was the pursuit of education. I already had a bachelor's degree, but that was not enough. At that time, acquiring wealth or fame, getting into a business, or buying a huge house in the United States weren't in my list of priorities. My priority list was family, education, and a good job.

All I knew was that I wanted to get into that classroom so bad and keep learning. Daddy had told me as a teenager he had no savings accounts or investments for my future, but he was willing to send me to school, that education was his investment for his children. I did not quite understand him then as I do now. Of all my years of living, thirty- one years have been spent in a classroom setting or learning something, and I always tell myself I got out of my mother's womb, ran into the classroom, and have been there ever since.

It amazes me that in developed countries where you do not have to walk ten miles to a classroom or bathe in the river, we have children dropping out of high school. Instead of carrying books to school, some children carry drugs or a weapon. Scholarships for college, student loans, grants, or online classrooms are readily available. Why would some children not use these opportunities? And you are also tempted to ask, where are their parents and what happened to parenting and responsibility? Often, the teachers take the blame when we all know that charity always begins in the home.

There are more than enough books to go around, and computers and libraries are well equipped. There is running water and enough bathrooms for kids at school, to say the least. No one calculates math on the hot sand outside, as do some kids in the developing countries, most of whom have no knowledge of a chalkboard, computers, or a calculator, besides having no books to read! For the most part, there is food for nourishment of those brains in developed countries, which some children in other parts of the world yearn for.

In some developing countries, children use outdoor latrines where the maggots meet you at the doorstep and crawl on your shoes, if you have shoes at all, or your bare feet. When you get out of this kind of a toilet, you stink of feces for the remainder of the day.

Electricity is readily available in most developed countries, reminding me of some eighth graders back in Kenya trying to study with lanterns or candle light at night, some just praying for a full moon to review a sentence. Some people give excuses about things that happened before they were born, when they are in the here and the now. Hopefully, our forefathers are resting in peace.

Some people are so fortunate that those before them paved the way for their freedom at all costs, so when you have some freedom, do not complain. Some woman in the world somewhere has none; she has to cover her body day and night and may never have the opportunity to learn. Remember, those before you worked hard, and whatever their circumstances, they somehow overcame, and I do not think they would have empathy for those giving excuses amidst tons of endless opportunities.

There would literally have been no life for me as a woman in a continent considered so poor, where winning a lottery or gambling is not an option, had I not listened to my dad. I personally believe in success through hard work. I probably would have been married with six kids, with poverty looming over ever step I took, but Daddy knew the value of education and as an educated man, he wanted the best for his children.

Mine was a family of thirteen children with no college funds, and no government loans or scholarships, only a dad who worked hard because Mama gave up her nursing career to care for us. Thankfully, we did not have to walk ten miles to school. We did not know drugs, race, or hatred to blame for not attaining education or successful careers. Most African countries are also ravaged by civil wars in addition to poverty, disease, and lack of opportunities for prosperity, which are genuine concerns and not excuses.

Currently, it is so hard in most African countries to go to college or even find a decent job. Those who have gone to college made it mainly through contributions from friends and family. My contributors were solely my parents and siblings. I went to an expensive private college in Kenya right after Daddy retired, and so it was harder for me than most of my older siblings, but I held on because *giving up* or *dropping out* was not in our family vocabulary. Dad was willing to sacrifice his retirement money and his material possessions for my future. Thank you, Dad!

I watched my father sell some of his land, a mini van, and even livestock for my tuition. At one time desperate to assist my dad, I asked the college if I could wash and press the one hundred choir robes, myself being a member of that choir, and as it turned out, I earned some good money from that.

When college was in recess, I went to a local market at the village back home to sell used magazines, some of my sisters begging me to stop because they thought that was embarrassing to the family, my father having been an accountant for years, a staunch Christian, and popular. I started my career at a nursing home when I first came to America and thankfully learned lessons about humility. As the wise counsel of Solomon instructs, *"Whatever your hands find to do, do it with your might; for there is no work or device or knowledge or wisdom in the grave where you are going"* (Ecclesiastes 9:10) NKJV.

Before completing my studies in Kenya, I was engaged to be married to a theology student who was also eager to study. Our enthusiasm for education was the main reason for coming to America. I said to myself, If Carson D made it to become one of the world's best neurosurgeons, I was going to make it, since my middle name did not begin with a "D" and my God's name began with a capital G.

In my chemistry classroom in Michigan, thirteen students were enrolled, and of the thirteen students, I was the only African in this classroom, and then there was one African American who dropped the class in less than a week. So here I was, one black woman with eleven Caucasians in a class. Some of them were nice, and the others you wouldn't care to know.

I was pregnant, too, adding to how different I now looked, and I had an accent. I felt all alone, but when we took our first test, I got an A, and I said to myself, *Chemistry is not one of my favorite subjects, but I'm going to study like I've never studied before, and nobody is going to look at me like I just came from Pluto.* Some had idiosyncrasies that were ominous, but I chose to pay attention to the teacher.

The second and third tests got the instructor talking. All my formulas were right, and she said, "Eucabeth, you are so good in this subject; you may want to consider teaching chemistry." And I smiled, gaining enough motivation and momentum from my instructor to last me for the rest of the semester, with an A all the way. As for teaching chemistry, it will never happen; God knows I studied for the purpose of passing the class, period! So I asked Him, and He pumped my brain with intellect.

Accent or no accent, with English as a second language, I was going to become the captain of the ship, and no one would stop me. A good attitude makes do what you imagine impossible. At least I knew I did not have an excuse or a bad attitude to blame. Here was an opportunity to learn, and I had to strive for the best. I was in America, where opportunity presents itself to the willing.

I was not just going to be sitting in an American classroom but doing some serious learning as well. I cared less for the next student looking at me with a grin. And my teacher, who was not African by any means, and looked completely different than I did, only gave me the grade I worked so hard for. As a human being, I truly felt like a Yankee after working so hard and beating all odds in my chemistry classroom. I had worked hard and deserved it, and still did not forget to give all the credit to my creator.

An African girl sitting in an American classroom with the God of possibility in her mind, I now owned the keys that unlocked the doors to the chemistry world, at least for that time. No one denied me this opportunity; it was available. I have so far been disappointed that most students do not take the college in their own backyard seriously and let the legal, and some illegal immigrants walk right through those classroom doors while they watch.

It is indeed sad to hear people say at many graduation ceremonies in developed countries, "I was the first in my family to graduate." Of course the tessellating pieces of information of formal education are often a rigorous experience, but who said the same pieces in a jigsaw puzzle cannot be completed in a classroom setting? Can we not put together the same pieces for our lives without assuming they are mountains we cannot climb?

Opportunities Unlimited

The unlimited opportunities in America are not served up on a platter or on anyone's doorsteps. One has to be willing to go and fetch these opportunities, and each willing spirit and soul has these opportunities available for exploration. Most celebrities can tell you they worked hard and for long hours for their achievements. They did not wake up one day to find themselves on the big screen.

Seeing an opportunity and grabbing it to better your life is up to you! Many people have made life easier for themselves using their God- given talents. They figured they could talk, and talk well, and after the years of hard work, talking and making some sense, they deserve their millions.

Some young men and women figured real estate was their adventure. They worked hard and progressed beyond expectations, and this kind of progressive thinking makes our communities better places. Seeing such people stepping up to uplift their communities, or getting involved in charitable organizations is encouraging. The sad fact is that some people take opportunity for granted! *Opportunity* is a term that does not resonate in the rest of the world as it does in the United States of America.

Education was costly for me, but the value of education outweighs how much you owe in government student loans. Some financial experts say that educational loans are good loans, and you know what, I'm paying these loans back diligently. The satisfaction I felt from attaining the knowledge far outweighed the cost, and learning that I could do much more with the knowledge obtained gave me a reason to keep studying. There was no way of getting such loans in Kenya to obtain an education. My loan office in Kenya was Daddy's wallet, which was now in retirement, but I did not have to repay him anything, thankfully.

Education provides you with a sense of security and no uncertainties. I've yet to see doctors or nurses laid off jobs. Thankfully, I can put food on the table each day, and my children do not have to open an empty fridge or worry about their next meal, which has nothing to do with luck and everything to do with hard work. My children have some decent clothing on their backs because of a good dream, opportunity, and hard work. Above all, they are healthy and happy, and I am, too.

After seeing all the malnourished children in Africa, I did not dare come to America and waste any time. I made my standard of living different. Struggling and partly surviving was not part of that dream.

Would you choose to raise beggars or thieves when two hands, two feet, a brain, and living in a developed country are your options? A degree holds lots more value in the current economic trends, despite the depreciation in value of the dollar, home foreclosures, and rising oil prices, depending on your career choice.

When you look at your paycheck as a graduate, depending on your area of expertise, you can be almost certain you are going to pay that mortgage or have food on the table for your family, and not sit in the streets of a developed country or work some low- paying job illegally.

You can also afford to buy a reliable car that can take you to and from work, and fill that gas tank without shivering. Of course, there are middle- class Americans barely surviving on two jobs, according to some news anchors, due to the economy, and I think their career path has a lot to do with working two jobs. When I came to America, I knew my potential was not limited to figuring out how many calories are in a packet of cookies as a nutritionist.

As human beings, we often limit ourselves where God has not limited us. I knew I was a caring being and had some compassion, and if I can serve a meal with these same two positive components of a human life, I could be good in the health care arena, where compassion and caring are key ingredients for service, and nurses are not easily laid off. *The sky is the limit*, as someone once said, and so I could be a nurse today or a doctor in a few more years, because personally, my limit is beyond the sky. Think beyond the sky! This is a possibility in America.

As a graduate nurse, I have participated in studies on the global nursing shortage, and was stunned at the staggering numbers of nurses being shipped in from other countries, to the United States, and Britain. When you visit most American hospitals, it is so easy to identify the overwhelming number of doctors named Guptahh and Olajwon or the staggering numbers of Filipino, Kenyan, and Nigerian nurses who have been offered jobs in the United States.

So then, one can precisely say that there are a lot of legal immigrants in this country who are contributing to the economy as well as positively making a difference in the communities in which they live. They did not have to cross the Mexican border to work for American farmers or industries illegally.

It has been over a decade since my husband lifted heavy pots and pans in the college cafeteria for a minimum wage that would never rise. Such is the experience that uplifts you or can destroy you if you let it. I'm glad he now has an office where he can provide some counseling to soldiers as a chaplain with the United States Army. Did he steal anyone's dream? No! He believed he could dream, and is living his dream.

He can play all the golf he wants and drive a car of his choice, having walked barefoot as a child. I know my eleven- year- old son can look up to his daddy and say, "Hey, you are the man!" Hopefully, my daughters will look back and say, "Dad and Mom did the best they could for us. Hard work pays off!" That is the lesson I want my children to learn. And I hope they never to forget the God who put their hands and feet in place. *"Before I formed you in the womb I knew you; before you were born I sanctified you"* (Jeremiah 1:5) NKJV.

Tito and his wife, Lana, have lived in the United States for quite a while. Tito serves in the United States Army as a captain, and most people ask how he got in the army. "Were you recruited from Africa? Some people have asked." There are many more Africans, Asians, and Hispanics serving in the military. Many legal immigrants who have worked hard in this country are living their dreams as successful entrepreneurs, businessmen, professors, etcetera, and that should not startle anyone.

They made the most of opportunity in a relatively peaceful country where freedom still prevails. It is not just the world we live in that holds us accountable for what we do, heaven does, too. Our actions are judged in both places.

In my perspective, working hard does not only mean working three jobs on a minimum wage and living in the unknown for the rest of life. I have worked two jobs previously, and it is hard on your physical, spiritual, and mental well- being, and hard on your family, if you are raising one. Some people live their lives on luck, and those who have won lotteries can tell you that it did not last. It was gone with the wind, and like the twinkling of an eye, they found themselves in the world of the have-nots or homeless.

When you obtain knowledge, it gives you satisfaction and a sense of security. You do not have to be extremely wealthy to live a good life. A good education and one good job is all it takes sometimes. Still, there are hard working people who just do not seem to make ends meet, and sometimes it has a lot to do with the choices they make or the skills they acquire.

The problem I have is when someone tells me that they have worked as a nursing assistant for thirty years in the same nursing home with no progress. That, I think, is a long time, long enough to be teaching as a nursing instructor in a college setting. You can only lose your knowledge when you lose your mind, and it does not happen often.

As a successful medical doctor, Mamji, originally from an African country, is giving back to the community, and assisting brothers and sisters in the Diaspora. There were days I could work sixteen long hours almost every day of the week because I had a project to fulfill. The project was to assist my parents by building a house of their dreams. It took longer than expected, but they now live in a beautiful house. On the African continent, we are taught to give back, and I take pleasure in reaching out to those in need, either by assisting with tuition or pocket money or by sending money for food and clothing, or contributing to church projects. I do not have to be a celebrity or part of a charity organization to assist people.

My parents are retired, and it does not matter to me that there are so many of their children who can assist them. I send them money every month for their upkeep, and it brings me great joy that Daddy does not have to struggle in his old age. They can both sit back and enjoy their graceful years together. After all, they gave up everything for my siblings and me.

In my senior year in nursing school, I conceived our third child. We were not preparing for a child at that time, but there I was with two small children and a third one on the way. Yes, someone could say, "Well why bother? Drop off school and pick it up later." But I dread the world of procrastinators, of picking up later. It does not work well for me. The fact is- it is easier said than done by someone who does not put food on your table.

When I was very pregnant, my college adviser asked me if I would consider coming back another semester, but I knew in my heart that no one was going to limit my determination or potential to complete this race I had began on my own. If I had to give birth in class, that was going to be my last straw. I had already struggled enough, and this was my final semester before graduation. I told myself I was going to make it; it was my jigsaw puzzle and no one was going to place the pieces except me.

I went to class each day, and for nurses who know those long clinical hours at the hospital, I was there too. My baby decided to come on a Saturday, and on Sunday morning, I asked my husband to bring my textbooks to the hospital so I could study for a final exam scheduled on Monday. I went home Sunday evening and continued to study till the wee hours of the morning, nursing the baby and changing diapers in between. At eight o'clock Monday morning, I sat in class with the other students and took my test. Failure was not an option, so there was no "if I fail." It was "I am passing this test right now; help me, Lord!"

At the graduation ceremony in May of that year, one student came to me and told me, "Eucabeth, of all the people who graduated today, you are the only one who really graduated." She had seen me struggle with the responsibilities before me at that time, and in all my humility, I was an inspiration to her. She is now a nurse, as well, and raising her own family, too. Two years later, I embarked on graduate studies, which I completed successfully, enabling me to join the International Honor Society of Nursing. I'm still looking forward to completing my doctoral studies in health sciences, which is underway. I keep living my American dreams.

When you can come from a foreign country to America to get a good education, a reliable job, and medical coverage, and give back to the community, you have made good use of some of the opportunities, and your time in life. It is the opposite of doing drugs or running around with some worthless man who ends up in jail, making you a single mom on welfare.

It might not be one smooth road to success, but you go through the hassles and untangle these opportunities for yourself. It takes courage, determination, self-motivation, focus, and sometimes prayers to achieve your goals, making this short life sweeter for yourself and those around you.

No Excuses!

People give the excuse of having an accent for not getting a job, forgetting that we have a governor with a rich, thick accent, or they just blame past historical events. Even birds of the air look for food, don't they? And why should some young woman have five children by the time she is twenty years old just because there is governmental assistance?

Who is providing some guidance and counseling, or does it not matter? Aren't these the same people we ignore sometimes, the ones who come to rob our homes or kill us? If I'm not a role model or mentor to my own children, why should I expect them to become something great?

To live in a five- thousand- square- foot home, you have to dream about it and plan for it. The same applies to if you want to eat some fresh strawberries for breakfast without relying on anybody's but your own sweat. It is called hard work for those who have two hands and feet and are not crippled by any means. It is pitiful that even in adulthood, most people have not made a choice to obtain a good education, and some choose to work in restaurants for thirty years before considering a college education. By then, the tuition is unbelievably costly, there are children and sometimes grandchildren, and the list of miseries is endless. Then they curse the same God who put those hands and feet in place.

I have had some bad experiences, too, but I did not let these particular experiences get in my way or affect my dreams. As a nursing student, one of the male faculty members told me, on a clinical rotation day at a local nursing home in Michigan, "Eucabeth, you ought to think like a white middle- class American. You see, even in this nursing home, there is only one black nurse at that nurses' station." I would be glad to report to him fifteen years later that this country has been good to me, and I have been good to me, too. The God I serve has never left my side either, and I have since become middle class, and an American.

The blood in my veins does not flow in the opposite direction, and I'm still a human being regardless of my color. I have worked hard enough to achieve my purpose in life: serving others. It was an exciting and exhilarating experience as I drove to the voting venue, to vote for an American president for the first time, a president whose father is from my country, Kenya, and with whom I share a language, and a lineage.

When I went in for the swearing of the oath of allegiance, it was about the United States accepting me for who I am and have always been. I will take this oath seriously till I go to my grave. No one has denied me a job because of my origin, color, accent, or gender, and for that I'm grateful. At least my job has no color to it, and I love nursing.

Recently, I found myself as the only graduate nurse working at a particular health facility. I raised some concerns for the well- being of the patients, and the staff's safety. The nurses were being asked to rotate as nursing assistants, and when my turn came, I asked the charge nurse why. To make it worse, I was told I was going to work as a nursing assistant under a licensed practical nurse (LPN), which according to the nurse practice acts for the state in which I was employed at that time, was not acceptable.

I had my master's degree and someone was not happy, wanting to undermine my capabilities and my education because my resume was beefy. I had been a nursing assistant fifteen years ago, and after working so hard and achieving some academic success; someone still wanted me to use my skills as a nurse's aide instead of caring for the very sick or educating other nurses.

Most of the patients knew I was an excellent nurse, and so did the nurses. Some patients made requests when I was on duty that they would like to have me as their nurse. When I first started working at this health care facility, I was told the nurses argued one night about whether I was a registered nurse or a licensed practical nurse because I was black and from Africa. Well, they finally figured out who I was.

Since then, God has opened doors for even greener pastures, and I'm one grateful human being. Remember, experiences are for a life time, and we learn a lot from them, good or bad. My experience of moving from Africa to America is still continuing, and I do not take any experiences I go through in life lightly. I am still positively dreaming, and I believe you can positively dream, too.

Made in the USA
Charleston, SC
14 September 2010